D1212997

LOST TREASURE TRAILS

THOMAS PENFIELD

LOST TREASURE TRAILS

ILLUSTRATED BY ROBERT GLAUBKE

NEW YORK Grosset & Dunlap PUBLISHERS

CONTENTS

1. BURIED TREASURE! 3
2. THE SOURCES OF HIDDEN TREASURE 7
3. PEOPLE DO FIND BURIED TREASURE 11
4. TREASURE TROVE LAW 18
5. AMERICA'S FIRST TREASURE HUNTERS 21
6. THE SPANISH TREASURES OF THE SOUTHWEST 25
7. SPANISH GALLEONS AND THE TREASURE FLEETS 29
8. SUNKEN TREASURE SHIPS 33
9. PIRATES AND PIRATE TREASURE 37
10. THE BURIED TREASURE OF CAPTAIN KIDD 40
11. THE BURIED TREASURE OF JEAN LAFITTE 47
12. BLACKBEARD'S BURIED TREASURE 51
13. THE BURIED TREASURE OF BILLY BOWLEGS 55
14. LOST MINES 58
15. THE LOST BLUE BUCKET MINE 62
16. SEMINOLE BILL'S LOST MINE 67
17. THE LOST CABIN MINE 70
18. THE LOST LAKE OF GOLD 73
19. BURNT WAGONS AND BURIED TREASURE 78
20. STAGECOACHES AND HOLDUPS 83
21. THE BURIED TREASURE OF OLD IRONSIDES 86
22. OUTLAWS AND THEIR TREASURE 89
23. THE BURIED TREASURE OF SKELETON CANYON 94

CONTENTS

24. THE BURIED TREASURE OF COLOSSAL CAVE — 99

25. THE GREAT TRAIN ROBBERY TREASURE — 103

26. HENRY GORDIER'S LOST TREASURE — 107

27. MAXIMILIAN'S BURIED TREASURE — 111

28. KARL STEINHEIMER'S BURIED MILLIONS — 115

29. BARON CASTINE'S BURIED TREASURE — 119

30. THE BURIED TREASURES OF NEW ENGLAND — 122

31. PLANTATION TREASURES OF LOUISIANA — 127

32. THE BURIED TREASURE OF PADRE ISLAND — 130

33. THE BURIED TREASURES OF FLORIDA — 134

34. THE GREATEST TREASURE OF THEM ALL — 137

35. TREASURE CODE AND SIGNS — 140

36. GUIDE TO HIDDEN TREASURE IN THE UNITED STATES AND ITS WATERS — 142

    Sunken Ships — 142

    Lost Mines — 143

    Buried Treasure — 146

LOST TREASURE TRAILS

1.

BURIED TREASURE!

You push the spade into the earth again. You listen intently for the metallic sound which will tell you that you've found it!

You have been digging half the night and your back aches like fury. Around you the pile of fresh earth mounts as you probe deeper and deeper for the treasure you are certain is there.

You crawl out of the pit and sit down to rest. The moon floats lazily across a cloudless sky. The wind rustles lightly through the leaves. You listen to the strange night sounds—the scurrying of a nocturnal rodent, the swishing flight of a night bird, the baying of dogs in the distance.

Above you and all around you the night is outlined in shadowy, shapeless forms. What was that? You crouch to the earth and listen, but all you can hear is the thump, thump, thumping of your own heartbeat.

Your blood tingles with excitement! Could you have been followed? You have taken every precaution and you have kept your secret well. You finally realize that your imagination has been playing tricks on you. You go back to work.

Dig! Dig! Dig! There is treasure below—gold in an iron chest! Your mind runs wild. Your spade bites into the earth. Clang! It hits something hard. Steel or stone? You make the earth fly with every ounce of your strength.

Can this be it at last? You pry it loose and examine it carefully. It is a foot-long iron rod with a U-shaped end, crusted with rust and corroded with the years, but you recognize it at once. It is a kingpin from stagecoach days! You are on the right track! Surely, this is the clue you are seeking!

Your mind wanders and you find yourself living the treasure story that has brought you to this lonely mountain spot.

Seventy-five years ago, when the clatter of the stagecoach was a familiar sound throughout all the West wherever there wasn't a railroad, the scene of your present feverish digging was but a scant half mile from a stage route.

Once a week a treasure express left a mining camp—long since abandoned—and, guarded by carefully-selected armed men, hauled the week's bullion to Sacramento.

On this particular trip the stage driver was none other than weather-beaten old Gene Locke who had forgotten more about staging than most men ever knew. Riding on the box beside him was the king of the "shotgun messengers," Charley Byers, whose twinkling blue eyes and perpetual smile revealed little of his ferocious nature when aroused.

Inside the coach, astraddle the iron treasure chest, sat two more guards, armed to the teeth. At a signal from the station master, the treasure express rumbled away in a cloud of dust.

Such an array of gun talent was calculated to discourage the boldest highwayman and, indeed, it had for many months. But there is always someone who will tackle anything if the reward is sufficient. Such was the case on this day, and the stage was headed pell-mell for plenty of trouble and tragedy.

Slashing around a curve on a narrow ledge of mountain road, the lead horses were suddenly

dropped in their tracks by a thundering volley of gunfire from the rocks above. The careening stage ground to a stop.

The battle was short and furious, with the odds against the surprised treasure guards from the start. Within minutes the driver and top-messenger were dropped from their seat atop the stage. The two inside guards held off the bandits for a little while, but one by one they, too, were picked off.

While two of the bandits dragged the heavy treasure chest from the stage, the third pulled the kingpin from the doubletrees and released the surviving horses. All hands then set about trying to open the strongbox, but neither gunfire nor blows from the kingpin would crack the heavy lock.

Finally, concluding that reinforcements would be needed to open the chest, the bandits dragged it to a small ravine a half mile or so from the road. Here the chest was hurriedly buried and a rough map was made of the identifying landmarks.

A few days later, while gathering reinforcements in Sacramento, two of the highwaymen were killed in a gun battle, and the third was seriously wounded. The "reinforcements" were horses belonging to someone else, and in the West of those days, horse stealing was one of the worst crimes a man could commit.

The wounded bandit confessed the stage robbery, but stubbornly refused to reveal the hiding place of the treasure chest. Before he died in jail a friend visited him, and in his last breaths he gasped out that the chest was buried at the center of a triangle formed by three ash trees in a small ravine, and that the exact spot was marked by a kingpin stuck in the ground directly above the treasure.

Before the friend could get around to recovering the treasure, he, too, got mixed up with the law and served three years in jail. Shortly after his release he was killed in a gunfight, but he had told the story of the treasure to a pal.

Finally, the story of the buried chest became

more or less common knowledge—half truth, half legend—and many searches were made for the lost tell-tale kingpin. And then you became interested in the story.

You gathered all the facts you could lay your hands on. You talked to a lot of old-timers. You delved into books and records. You determined beyond a doubt that the stage was really held up and that it was carrying treasure. You slowly located the old stage route and you followed it mile after mile, seeking the spot most likely to have been the scene of the robbery.

You located an old stagecoach exactly like the one used by the stage line, and you knew exactly what the lost kingpin looked like. Old records revealed that there had been $240,000 in gold in that treasure chest, and you knew the exact dimensions of the chest—its width, height, and depth!

And then you found what you believed to be the site of the buried treasure! After all these years only one ash tree was still standing, but you found the stumps of two more and they formed a perfect triangle in a small ravine about a half mile from the site of the holdup.

You measured and remeasured until you found the exact center of the triangle—but there was no kingpin! You scraped at the earth, but it appeared as solid and as undisturbed as the day it was created. You retraced your steps, but they brought you to the same conclusion—the treasure is buried here!

You finally reasoned that the kingpin could have long since disappeared, perhaps picked up by a curious, unsuspecting horseman; perhaps covered by the years' accumulation of debris—a cloudburst, an earthquake. You could think of a thousand things that could have happened to that kingpin!

You carefully marked the spot until you could return with digging tools, and then one night you sneaked back to the treasure site, careful not to be followed. And here you are!

You tremble with every spadeful of earth you remove from the yawning pit. You imagine that you see faint marks of rust—and then you hit it! You know by the sound of the spade on solid metal that you have found the loot of the treasure-express holdup! You have found buried treasure!

2.

THE SOURCES OF HIDDEN TREASURE

Gold! What magic there is in that four-letter word. How many men has it sent into the Arctic wastes, to the burning deserts. Men of all ages have lived for it, fought for it, died for it.

Wherever buried treasure exists—and it is every place—anyone may hope to find it—a man or a child. The appeal is universal. None escapes its lure. It is in Maine, it is in California, it is in Florida—no matter where you live there is a story of buried treasure near you. How did it get there? Well, in many ways.

The Spanish explorers first came to North America in search of the fabulous treasure of the Seven Cities of Cibola. They found no treasure—only the mud hovels of the Zuni Indians, but they left behind them countless legends of buried treasure and lost mines.

Then came the mission padres, those brave men who traveled the inhospitable desert wastes to bring Christianity to the half-savages of the New World. Friendly and converted Indians brought in gifts of gold, and soon many of the early missions added mining to their amazing list of activities. Some of these mines, like the fabulous Taiopa of southern Arizona or northern Sonora, produced enormous quantities of ore, and even under the crude mining methods of the time, great piles of gold and silver were accumulated.

One by one the missions were raided by less friendly Indians, their property destroyed and their inhabitants killed or driven away. In escaping, there was no time to bother with treasure. It was concealed and left behind. This is the origin of many of the lost treasure stories of Arizona, New Mexico, California, and Nevada.

There is, for example, some reason to believe that part of the padres' treasure buried at the old mission of Tumacacori, Arizona, has been found. No less than two lost mines are connected with the Mission San Xavier del Bac, still standing near Tucson, and even the ruins of old Guevavi, near Nogales, are still poked through by eager treasure hunters.

Most of the treasure stories of the East Coast of the United States, of Florida, and the Gulf

Coast are connected with pirates, who, it seems, always had great chests of gold and silver to bury. There were, indeed, many pirates and they captured great quantities of treasure. What else could they do with it but bury it on some lonely island or deserted shore?

Blackbeard is said to have improved upon this system by killing all the crew who helped bury the treasure. At least one of the bodies would be thrown into the pit on top of the treasure chest in the superstitious belief that the skeleton would guard the treasure.

Between the years 1820 and 1830 it is said that a small army of some 2000 pirates were in operation in the Caribbean Sea alone, and that the cargoes they captured exceeded $20,000,000 in value. Many of these men sailing under the Jolly Roger made frequent trips to the shores of the United States.

The pirates' banking system was a cave or a hole in the ground. They picked out an island, a peninsula, or a cove and there dug a treasure pit. Landmarks were noted, a map drawn, and they sailed away in search of even more loot.

There is hardly a cove or an offshore island from Maine to the tip of Florida without its treasure story of Captain Kidd, Blackbeard, John Quelch, or others equally infamous.

Florida! Well, there is the real treasure land— a natural haunt for pirates—Johnny Bowlegs, Black Caesar, Gasparilla, and a host of others who preferred the security of the soil of Florida!

Around the Gulf from Key West to Corpus Christi the treasure of Jean Lafitte is sought in a score or more of places, especially near the mouth of the Nueces River in Texas.

Sunken ships contribute a great number of stories to the vast treasure lore of the United States. It is estimated that the value of the treasure cargoes wrecked on the shores of Florida alone amounts to $170,000,000, and from Maine to Puget Sound there is no stretch of with gold and silver, sailed up past the Florida coast on their way to the Old World, the Spanish seamen never seemed to learn that June to December was hurricane season. Many a proud vessel ended her voyage on a Florida beach or was blown clear across the Gulf to pile up on

shoreline without its special treasure story.

Sunken ships are easy to authenticate, not always so easy to locate. They are likely to sink in the silt of the ocean's bed, to shift with the strong undercurrents, and to break apart. Nevertheless, many sunken ships have been found by treasure seekers and their cargoes recovered.

Many of the buried treasures of Florida and the Gulf Coast have their origin in the Spanish ships that carried the wealth of South America and Mexico to Spain. Although each year for many years two great fleets, their hulks loaded the sands of Padre Island below Corpus Christi.

Eager Indians waited on the shores, ready to salvage the wreckage and capture the survivors. Casks were broken open on the coarse white sands and gold coins would spill out to be ground under indifferent heels. Gold in bars, great kegs of silver ingots, bags of emeralds, rings, bracelets, streams of pearls, silver plate, gold candlesticks, cups and trays, crucifixes, jeweled combs, sacks of gold dust—all the treasures of Montezuma not already melted down would be left carelessly on the beach for the children to play with! Not until the Indians learned that the white man coveted the treasure and would fight for it, did they bother to bury the loot.

Throughout the entire West—wherever there were stagecoaches—there are stories of buried treasure. In a day when the six-gun was the only law, the problem of transporting the hundreds of millions of dollars taken from the mines of California, Nevada, Arizona, and South Dakota was left to the stage lines, who did a fine job.

In the single year of 1863, the Pioneer Stage Line, running between Genoa, Nevada, and Placerville, California, carried $12,000,000 worth of gold bullion in stagecoaches! And this was only one small line. There were many larger.

Bandits preyed upon the stages at every turn in the road, and to thwart them the stage lines had to employ every conceivable trick. Some of the stage lines used a specially constructed "treasure stage," which was virtually an armored vehicle. No passengers were carried and their drivers were selected for their reputation and resourcefulness. They were the heroes of their age and the idols of every small boy.

A guard sat atop the dickey seat with the driver, a revolver in each hand, cocked and ready to shoot. If the treasure was particularly rich, two guards would ride inside the stage, armed to the teeth and ready for anything.

Although the vast bulk of the gold and silver dust and bullion carried by the stagecoaches reached its destination, there were many successful robberies and these are the basis for many buried treasure stories in the West.

Out of the mining camps of the West grew the hundreds of tales of "lost mines" and many of these stories have a basis in fact. They follow pretty much the same pattern. Two old prospectors find a rich ledge. Their water supply gives out, or they are surprised and driven away by Indians. They are never quite able to find their way back to the ledge where "basketsful of nuggets lay big as goose eggs!"

Some of these "mines" were actually lost, and some have been found again, like the Lost Wheelbarrow Mine in Washington. Some have grown into fabulous stories, like the Lost Dutchman Mine in the Superstition Mountains of Arizona. Dozens of lives have been lost in the ceaseless search for the Lost Dutchman.

In the South many of the treasure stories are a result of the War between the States. When the cry "The Yankees are coming!" swept the country, many families hurried to bury their wealth lest it fall into the hands of the invaders. Much of this treasure has never been recovered, and throughout the former Confederacy almost every community has its treasure story.

Bandit loot from holdups and robberies is buried throughout the country. Buried in the haste of flight, for one reason or another many of these secret caches were never recovered. A good example is the suitcase containing a million dollars buried by the John Dillinger gang near Rhinelander, Wisconsin. Before any of the mob could return to recover the treasure, they were all rounded up by the G-men.

Probably the greatest sources of buried treasure are the private hoards buried all over the nation. Before the days of banks, the ground was considered the safest place for wealth of all kinds. But even after banks came into being, many people still hid their wealth in a pot or an old tin can.

My grandfather used to tell of the time when, early one autumn morning, his father sneaked into the woods near Eaton, Ohio, carrying an iron pot full of gold coins. With boyish curiosity Grandfather followed him but his little dog barked and he was sent back to the house. Sometime later his father was killed by the Indians, and the secret of the treasure was never found.

Hundreds of private caches have been found —and more are found all the time—but countless hundreds still remain where their owners once placed them—and walked away.

Yes, there is buried treasure almost everywhere. It is hidden for many reasons, and the search for it goes on endlessly—in caves, in the walls of old buildings, in attics, in cellars, in the desert, in mountains, under rocks, and in the sea. Whether you are an amateur treasure hunter or a professional, it is great sport—even if you never find anything. But who knows? You may be the one who will.

3.

PEOPLE DO FIND BURIED TREASURE

WITH BURIED TREASURE scattered over every section of the United States, you might wonder why more of it isn't found. Indeed, a great deal of buried treasure *is* found—much more than we ever hear about. People who find buried treasure have a habit of keeping it to themselves, and each has his own particular reason for doing so, but there are probably two main reasons why many treasure finds are never reported.

In the first place, secrecy prevents a legal battle with others who might claim the treasure, and even though title to the treasure might eventually be granted the finder, its winning can be costly.

Secondly, there is a matter of income taxes which some people have a strong feeling against, especially when it comes to finding buried treasure. The way to avoid this is, obviously, to keep the find to one's self, and this is done in more cases than anyone knows about. This, however, is an evasion of the law and is punishable by fine and imprisonment. It isn't worth the risk!

There are many hundreds of instances of buried treasure being found, both by design and accident, but for each reported case, there are perhaps a dozen unreported. I have been told of someone living in Los Angeles who dug up a chest of gold stolen in a stage robbery in Washington. The chest and its contents remain hidden because the man is afraid to turn in the gold. The stage driver was killed in the holdup, and the man who recovered the treasure was a member of the outlaw gang committing the robbery.

Many years ago pots of old Spanish coins were dug up in Maine on Haskell Island and on a small island in the Sasanon River near Bath. Both treasures were found by farmers

11

while plowing a field, and both finds touched off a frenzy of excitement.

Buried treasure has been found on at least four different occasions on Kelly's Bluff along the Mississippi River at Dubuque, Iowa, buried there, it is presumed, by an eccentric miner. People still dig in the area for more treasure.

Nearly $100,000 was dug up on a farm in Oley Valley, Pennsylvania. In silver and gold coins, it was cached away in earthern crocks presumably by a wealthy recluse.

At Colebrook, New Hampshire, in 1942, Ben Lay and his son were walking on the beach and picked up an old silver coin. They probed about in the sand and found other old coins. Finally they uncovered the corner of a box sticking out of the sand. Prying it open, they found several thousand dollars in gold and silver pieces, their dates indicating that the treasure had been buried around 1850.

Dublin, New Hampshire, was the scene of another treasure find in 1934, when Harold B. Lane, an attorney, uncovered a bean pot full of ten- and twenty-dollar gold pieces. The treasure had been buried by Mrs. Agnes Parsons who had left a letter leading to its discovery.

One never knows what strange circumstances will lead to buried treasure. Take the case of John Wilson, a shiftless resident of Bailey Island, Maine. One day in 1840 he was duck-hunting on Elm Island in Casco Bay. While following a wounded bird, he stumbled into a kelp-covered hole in the rocks and, pulling aside the slippery seaweed to extricate himself, he pulled out an old copper kettle full of strange coins. For his inconvenience, John Wilson was $12,000 richer!

Around 1900 George Benner of Middlesex, Vermont, found an old map in an attic. The area covered on the map was recognized as Boothbay Harbor and the Kennebec River in Maine. Inscribed on it were these instructions:

Stand abrest qurtsbolder bring top in line with hill n½ m it lise 12 fathoms ne near big trees under stone

Benner secured a small boat and went to Boothbay Harbor with a companion. Some distance up the banks of the Kennebec they found an enormous quartz boulder. Although only one tree stood in the vicinity, the stumps of many others indicated that the area had once

been heavily wooded. With a crowbar, Benner poked into the ground until he hit something hard. When uncovered, this proved to be a large flat stone, and under this stone a second was found. They dug down several feet and finally uncovered a metal chest, its top rusted and caved in, but its contents still intact—several handfuls of gold and silver coins, a string of pearls, and a diamond-encrusted cross.

Florida has probably yielded more buried treasure than any other section of the United States. A man named Taylor unearthed a cache of Mexican coins worth $25,000 on Grassy Key, together with a golden candlestick and a diamond ring.

In 1913 a Pensacola contractor, Charles Villar, found a Spanish treasure chest in the shallow waters of Bayou Chico near Pensacola. The chest, undoubtedly placed there by pirates, contained several thousand dollars in gold and silver coins.

A Miami man, E. C. Cole, was digging a ditch on his property near the water when he came to some burned and rotted timbers. Exploring the area further, he dug up several pieces of melted metal which proved to be gold and silver. It was presumed that a ship had been wrecked and burned near there and that the coins had been fused together with the heat.

Ned Pent, a pilot, found a treasure chest in a group of mangroves near Cutler, Florida. The coins were Mexican and badly corroded, but worth several thousand dollars to the finder.

Another treasure chest was found near Jupiter Inlet, Florida, by an unknown party of men. A schooner was seen landing some men carrying surveying instruments in the mangroves north of the inlet. After two days of work, the men were seen to drag a heavy chest to the shore and load it in their boat. They sailed away, leaving a gaping hole, the bottom of which was clearly marked with the outline of a rusty chest. They must have found, by some means or other, an old treasure map!

Again, a man called "Alligator" Ferguson, for his occupation of catching alligators, consistently sold old Spanish coins to a Tampa bank, but refused to reveal anything except that he had found a Spanish treasure chest.

Another Spanish chest was found near Sarasota a few years ago after children playing in a group of mangroves brought home a few old coins and bits of rusted iron. A search in the vicinity revealed an old pirate chest that had been buried there many years before.

About 1930 Harry Gilbert was fishing on Lower Matecumbe Bay. While walking on the beach he found an old and rotted goatskin pouch which broke open at his touch. Out spilled some $80,000 in Spanish coins. A similar find, valued at $70,000, was made on Captain's Key.

Arthur McKee of Homestead City was searching the waters off Key Largo in 1949 for old Spanish cannon. He spotted a wrecked galleon on a coral reef and, being a diver himself, he went down and brought up three coral-encrusted silver ingots weighing about 70 pounds each. The Smithsonian Institute in Washington identified the bars as having come from a mine in Panama. McKee is certain that the three ingots are but a small portion of the treasure in the wreck.

One of the most recent and largest Florida treasure finds was reported in November 1953, when William F. Sneed, Jr., a Lakeland hotel operator, claimed to have found treasure at the mouth of the Suwannee River totaling 4500 gold pieces and 3500 of silver. The coins were in a chest which was located with an electronic device under 16 feet of water. Two treasure ships have long been searched for in the Suwannee, and Sneed may have found one of them.

Captain Josiah Merrill found a pirate treasure chest filled with gold coins on Pilot Island, Connecticut, at the entrance to Norwalk Harbor. He said the treasure had been revealed to him in three successive dreams!

Near Brawley, California, Thomas Moore found a cache of gold weighing between 50 and 60 pounds along the banks of the Alamo River, which is dry except during the rainy season. The gold had apparently been hidden many years earlier by bandits and was finally revealed by a caving-in of the river bank.

In April 1950, a bulldozer leveling off a vacant lot at Folsom, California, uncovered a can containing five-, ten-, and twenty-dollar gold pieces. The justice of the peace had to be called out to control the gold rush that resulted. The bulldozer operator was awarded one-half the treasure; the justice retained the rest!

In 1948 another vacant lot was being cleared at Monterey, California, for a new school building. A group of curious boys poking around in the dirt uncovered a can of gold coins valued at $6000. It is amazing how much treasure is actu-

ally uncovered by boys through their insatiable desire to explore and dig around in out-of-the-way places. It can pay to be curious!

Four World War I veterans gardening at Youngville Soldier's Home, Napa, California, unearthed a pot of gold coins in 1936. Immediately thereafter everybody at the Home wanted the garden assignment!

In 1942 Mario L. Bernardi of Yuba City, California, was planting a victory garden. His spade struck something hard which he pulled up and tossed aside. It was a can that burst revealing a considerable fortune in gold and silver coins.

The farm of Jim Hawkins in Huntsville, Arkansas, was the scene of a treasure hunt in 1925. Hawkins was thought to have been quite wealthy but no trace of his wealth was found until a can of gold coins was found buried under the porch. Later searchers found pots of coins hidden from one end of the farm to the other.

In 1933 the American Red Cross conducted a treasure hunt on a farm near Little Rock, Arkansas. The treasure had been buried by R. F. Leigh, an aged recluse who died rather than reveal the hiding place of his treasure. On December 29 Leigh's body was found hanging from a rafter in his house. Two youths were captured and confessed that they had killed the man in trying to force him to reveal where his treasure was hidden.

About a year before his death, Leigh had left a sealed envelope with a neighbor with instructions not to open it until his death. These directions were followed, and a year later the envelope was found to contain a second envelope addressed to the American Red Cross in Washington.

Red Cross officials were puzzled over the strange note inside but followed these directions:

Stand in the front of my house. Look just to the right of the northwest corner of the front post of the porch. Go about 50 yards to a wall of rock. In it you will find two boxes of money.

The treasure was recovered precisely according to instructions!

In 1926 buried treasure consisting of $200,-000 in gold coins was dug up on the Whitfield farm near Demopolis, Alabama, according to directions found in some old pre-Civil War documents. It pays to read those old papers!

Four young boys were playing cops and robbers in Florence, Alabama, in April 1942. One of the "robbers" dug a hole in which to bury the imaginary loot and uncovered a pot containing $5,850!

The $85,000 buried by stage robbers near Fort Huachuca, Arizona, was exposed by the blade of a plow in 1944, but the plowman failed to notice the corner of the rusty chest sticking up in the fresh furrow. A few days later Eldon Wallace, a boy of eleven at the time, was playing alone in the field. He found the chest but couldn't budge it. On the following day he returned to the field with a companion, and the two dug up the chest but it was too heavy for them to move nor could they pry it open. About this time the owner of the property, Lester Wade, appeared on the scene. He drove the boys away and took possession of the chest. Wallace just recently started court action to recover the treasure which he claims is rightfully his.

Alden Barnett was cutting trees in a wood just outside Millville, New Jersey, in 1908. His foot hit a wooden box covered with leaves and he stopped to investigate. Inside the box was a bag of gold and silver coins and several checks drawn on a bank in New York. This was no doubt the loot from a bank holdup, but Barnett was permitted to keep the coins.

In 1910 Dr. Joseph S. Wooten of Austin, Texas, found a musty piece of parchment while exploring a cavern in the Rio Grande region. The parchment proved to be a map of the Gulf Coast with all the lettering done in French. A cross marked the location of a buried chest of Jean Lafitte, the pirate, and was signed by Joni Benuit, one of his lieutenants.

Dr. Wooten spent several months following the Texas shore until he found a land contour that seemed to agree with the one on the map.

It was Matagorda Island, one of the long chain of sandy islands near Corpus Christi. With two other men as partners, Wooten made a minute search of the island and finally found two heavy chests containing $86,000 in gold and silver coins and a lot of almost worthless jewels and trinkets. There is little doubt but that this was part of the treasure of the famed Lafitte, and there is plenty more still to be found if but a tenth of the Lafitte buried-treasure legends are true.

A pirate chest was uncovered along the Tred Avon River near Easton, Maryland, in 1903 by Solomon Cooby. Near by the skeletons of several persons were found, and although the chest was said to have been buried by the pirate, Henry Morgan, this seems unlikely. Morgan's treasure was uncovered many years ago in Panama.

Jack Thornton was hunting mountain lions in northern Arizona. Fearing that a lion he had wounded might attack him, he scampered into a near-by cave. The wounded animal followed Thornton into the cave, but he was able to kill it. Something about the cavern aroused Thornton's curiosity and he decided to explore it. Following the course of the cave for some distance, he came upon a rotten board protruding from a pile of rock. This, Thornton reasoned, was evidence that someone had been here before him. One by one he pulled the stones aside and uncovered a wooden strong box. Inside the box were slabs, ingots, and chunks of virgin silver! The value of the silver later turned out to be about $50,000.

Who put the silver in the wooden box, covered it with rocks, and walked away? The question has never been satisfactorily answered, but the theory at the time was that the treasure had been hidden by men stealing the ore from a near-by mine—highgraders, they are called.

For many years a legend persisted around Cape Girardeau, Missouri, that there was buried treasure on the Bryce farm. No one really believed there was any truth in the story until Art Schwank, a rose fancier, rented a small piece of the Bryce property for a rose garden. One day while Schwank was digging away, his spade struck something hard. He pulled up a tin box and was $30,000 richer!

Two boys, Alfred and Thomas Nowak, were playing in the vacant mansion of a Yonkers, New York, recluse, when they found a small metal box containing $34,000. Finders were not keepers in this case, however, and the boys had to give up the treasure when it was established that the occupant had hidden it.

Another recluse, Miss Louise Herle, hid $525,750 in her Brooklyn home. Searchers found it after practically tearing the place down. However, it was thought that Miss Herle was worth $1,500,000 at the time of her death. The remainder has never been located.

In 1913 a laborer named George Hardsook was working in a field near Claremont, Oklahoma, when he found $37,000 in twenty-dollar gold pieces. Later on, Kit Dalton, supposedly a former member of the Jesse James gang, claimed that the money was part of a $70,000 train holdup at Mosscrest, Oklahoma. The gold had been buried near a tree, he said, but when the gang had returned to recover it they failed to locate any of the identifying landmarks.

A few years ago a Philadelphia bookkeeper found a cache of $92,800 in the basement of his home, but it brought him nothing but trouble. No fewer than twenty-eight different individuals and agencies claimed the treasure, including the Commonwealth of Pennsylvania and the United States government. A long court fight resulted, and the finder ended up in the hole!

Two cowboys uncovered a glass jar of gold coins in the cellar of an abandoned property in Rock Creek, Wyoming. A man named Taylor stepped up to claim the treasure, and the case was taken to court. The cowboys lost.

A cache worth $6000 was found in the basement of a house owned by R. C. Bennet at Eagle River, Wisconsin. The treasure was buried in about sixty separate tin boxes and was thought to be but a small portion of the treasure actually buried on the place. Mr. Bennet did not permit any more searching!

In 1929 Clyde Pickett of Baton Rouge, Louisiana, was searching the grounds of his ancestral home in Vicksburg for the family silverware supposedly buried during the Civil War. He failed to find the silver, but in a hole bored in an old oak tree he found a cache of gold and silver coins worth several thousand dollars.

Yes, buried treasure is found, both by people who are searching for it and by those who come across it by accident. Like gold, treasure is where you find it!

4.

TREASURE TROVE LAW

WITH BURIED TREASURE scattered all over the United States, what are your chances of keeping a secret cache you might find? Will you have to surrender it? Will you have to share it with someone? What about the owner of the land on which treasure is found? What about Uncle Sam?

In the first place, there are two facts that should be cleared up. The first is the definition of treasure trove; the second is the Gold Reserve Act of 1934 and its effect upon the finder of buried treasure.

Treasure trove is defined legally as gold or silver in plate, bullion, or coins, found in the ground or in a house, building, or other private place, for which no legal owner can be located. Note that the treasure must be found *in* the ground, not on top of it, and that it is in gold or silver plate, bullion, or coins, *not currency*. That is the definition of treasure trove.

The Gold Reserve Act of 1934 took out of public circulation all gold coins and currency (gold notes) and prohibited the private holding of gold bullion, coins, or notes except for use in jewelry, dentistry, and numismatic collections.

Now, according to the law, if you find treasure consisting of gold bullion, coins, or notes—no matter where you find it—you must surrender it to the Treasury Department of the United States. If your legal claim to the treasure is established and if there are no violations involved in the finding of the treasure, you will be reimbursed for the full value of the gold at the current rate. You may even be permitted to keep or to sell a limited quantity of certain gold coins for collection purposes.

If your find is made on Federal property you must also surrender it to the Treasury Department, but you may not be reimbursed for the full value regardless of whether it is gold or silver. You may not be reimbursed at all, for it is presumed that all treasure trove found on Federal property belongs to the public treasury. Usually, however, when it is established after a reasonable length of time that the rightful owner of the treasure cannot be located, the government is willing to share with you. The amount it is willing to share is entirely up to Treasury Department officials. They have usually been generous.

In any case, and this is most important, you must pay income taxes on *any* treasure found and established as belonging to you.

In England the title to all buried treasure rests in the Crown, which may grant all, or any part, to the finder. It may not grant any if it so desires. It is considered the duty of every finder of buried treasure in England immediately to report any find to the proper officials, and it is, furthermore, the duty of everyone having any knowledge of the finding of buried treasure to report the fact. Failure to do so in either case is an indictable offense. In actual practice, both in England and in the United States, treasure finders have been shared with generously by their governments.

In the United States, the common law of treasure trove follows the English pattern only in regard to treasure found on Federal property.

In 1947 Secretary of the Interior James A. Krug ruled that treasure found on Federal property under the jurisdiction of the Department of the Interior would belong to the finder provided that the finder *secured permission* from the proper agency to dig for the treasure. The decision was an outgrowth of a request from Ray B. Dean to search for treasure in the Wichita Mountains Wildlife Game Refuge in southwestern Oklahoma. Although there are several treasures reported buried in the Wichita Mountains, including the loot of the Jesse James gang, Dean did not report any success and a test was not made of the Secretary's ruling.

Different States have different laws regarding the disposition of treasure found on private property. In Louisiana, for example, it is generally assumed that the courts will divide any treasure between the finder of the treasure and the legal property owner on whose place the treasure was found. In other States the legal owner of the property on which the treasure is found has been denied any share in the treasure. In California the law is vague, and in some instances the courts have awarded all the treasure to the property owner and in others they have denied him of it altogether.

The finder of buried treasure on private property, therefore, may or may not have to share his find with the legal property owner, depending upon where he lives and the circumstances of his discovery. The safest course in any event is to attempt to secure the property owner's permission to search for treasure and to agree to a division of any treasure found. Owners of private property may, of course, deny anyone the privilege of trespassing on their property.

Municipalities may require you to post a bond to insure that you will repair any damage done while searching for treasure on public property, and they will usually insist upon a share of any treasure found. In at least two instances the city of Los Angeles has granted permission to search for treasure on city property, demanding in addition to the usual bond, a fifty-fifty division of any treasure found.

In most States if a group of people finds buried treasure, each person in the group shares equally in the treasure unless the partners have previously agreed upon another division. Each person in the party is also legally bound to keep intact his share of the treasure for a reasonable length of time in case the rightful owner of the treasure should appear and claim his property.

In 1907 three boys in New Vineyard, Massachusetts, were hired by a property owner to clean up the debris in his yard after a fire had damaged a small building. While scraping and digging around, one of the boys uncovered a rusty tin can. When he pulled the can from the ground, the bottom fell out and a shower of coins cascaded from it. Further search immediately uncovered two more cans, both filled with coins. The owner of the property took possession of the coins and placed them in his house for safekeeping. When it was time for the boys to leave, the property owner paid them off and refused them any share in the treasure on the grounds that it was found on his property.

A few days later the boys wondered if they were not entitled to a share of the treasure, and they were supported in this view by several citizens. An attorney filed suit, and weeks later the case came to trial. The judge ruled that the

the owner of the property stepped up and claimed the entire treasure. The parents of the boys refused to surrender the coins, and the case was taken to court. After a prolonged legal battle, during which no rightful owner of the treasure appeared, the court awarded the entire treasure to the boys on the old assumption that

coins had been buried by a person or persons unknown and, having, therefore, no legal owner, belonged to the finders. The property owner, however, happened to be present when the coins were found and was assumed to be one of the finders. The treasure was ordered divided in four shares. The point was made clear that the property owner would have received no share had he not been present when the coins were dug up.

In 1937 two Baltimore boys were playing in the cellar of a vacant house on South Eden Street. They were burying an imaginary treasure hoard when their shovels hit something hard. They uncovered an iron pot which, much to their amazement, was full of gold coins. As soon as news of the treasure find got around,

"finders are keepers" as long as legal ownership can not be proved.

Because of the legal battles that often follow the finding of buried treasure many people keep their find a close secret. This is why you don't hear of more treasure being found.

A safe set of rules to follow in hunting for buried treasure is: 1. Secure permission from the property owner to search on private property and arrange beforehand for a division of any treasure found. 2. Secure permission from the proper officials to hunt for buried treasure on public lands and, if possible, arrange for the division of any treasure found. 3. Surrender any gold found to the Treasury Department. 4. Report the value of your find to the Internal Revenue Bureau and pay your income taxes!

5.

AMERICA'S FIRST TREASURE HUNTERS

More than four hundred years ago, in 1536, a small party of Spanish soldiers was traveling through the wild mountain country along the Gulf of California in western Mexico. They were returning to their base at Culiacán, weary from the long march, when a strange and startling sight brought them to a sudden halt.

Ahead of them staggered four men. Three of the strangers, almost naked and hardly more than skeletons, appeared to be white. The fourth was dark and, some thought, black. All had long beards and their hair hung in matted knots. None could talk through swollen tongues that filled their mouths.

Exhausted, the four strangers fell at the feet of the amazed troops, hardly aware that they had at last found safety with their own countrymen. It was hours before the mystery of the four strangers could be pieced together. Finally one regained enough strength to gasp out the frightful story. His name was Alvár Núñez Cabeza de Vaca. His companions were Andres

Dorantes, Alonso de Castillo Maldonado—all Spaniards, and the fourth man, the swarthy one, was a Moor, Estevanico, the slave of Dorantes.

Where had they come from? How long had they traveled? Where was their ship? What were they looking for? The soldiers asked a thousand impatient questions at once. Slowly Cabeza de Vaca told their story.

They had left Spain in 1527—nine horrifying years before—as members of an expedition headed by Pánfilo de Narváez. Their instructions were to explore and colonize La Florida, far to the east. They had landed in a large sheltered bay on the west coast of Florida, but found the Indians most resentful of their presence.

After repeated attempts to subdue the Indians, the Spanish were attacked. Several of the Spaniards had been killed and others captured. Some had managed to reach the boats and sail away. For many days they had sailed along the Gulf Coast until a terrible storm came up. Unable to withstand the battering of the heavy

21

seas, their little vessel was tossed up on a strange shore. Only these four survived the wreck.

For eight horrible years they had wandered among the wild tribes, frequently held as slaves, always in danger of losing their lives at any second. Slowly they worked their way toward the setting sun, attacked by strange diseases, weakened by thirst and hunger, preyed upon by men and animals alike. Finally they had come to a land of friendly Indians who offered shelter and food. Here they remained a long time, regaining their strength and listening to the fantastic tales told by the sympathetic red men.

In a land known as Cibola, many leagues to the north, related the Indians, there were seven cities where the buildings were studded with jewels and the pots and pans were made of gold.

"Gold!" exclaimed the Spanish soldiers. "Cities of Gold!"

"Yes," answered Cabeza de Vaca, "but we were too weary to seek gold. We wanted only to escape with our lives."

When strong enough to travel again, the four men had left the friendly Indians and for many

months traveled southwestward across barren mountains and burning deserts, hoping always to reach the sea and perhaps a ship that would carry them home.

After several days of rest the four wanderers were able to travel and the soldiers took them to Mexico City where their story of the Seven Cities of Cibola could be related to the authorities. There would be rewards for all.

In the capital of New Spain, Cabeza de Vaca told the story to the viceroy himself, Antonio de Mendoza. "We must organize an expedition at once!" Mendoza exclaimed. "We must take the Seven Cities of Cibola, and all their riches, for the Crown of Spain!"

But it takes time to organize an expedition. Mendoza impatiently despatched a small exploratory party north under the command of a Franciscan friar, Marcos de Niza. In the meantime the main expeditionary forces would be organized and outfitted.

Marcos de Niza had some experience as an explorer and he was a man Mendoza thought could be trusted. He had been with Pizarro in Peru. His record was one of faithful and diligent service to his Church and country. Selected to accompany De Niza was another friar named Onorato, and the black Moor, Estevanico, was to go along as guide. He was now known to all as "Black Stephen."

De Niza's instructions were explicit. He was to find the Seven Cities of Cibola. If they were as rich as Cabeza de Vaca reported, he was to send Mendoza immediately a large cross to be carried in relays by Indian runners. If there was no treasure, the runners would carry a small cross.

In March 1539, De Niza and his small party started northward from western Sonora. For many days they traveled through the hot and inhospitable country. Onorato became ill and could no longer travel. De Niza remained with his ailing companion and the black man was sent ahead to scout the country.

Black Stephen, resplendent in brilliantly colored feathers and jingling bells, was received in awe by all the Indians he encountered. They wanted to touch him, but they did not harm the

nor by his fine regalia. At the village of Hawikuh they killed the black man.

Why had the Moor lied to De Niza? Perhaps
it was that he wished to be a hero and the first
to see the fabulous wealth of Cibola. He took
a chance that the story brought to Mexico by
Cabeza de Vaca was true and sent the cross
"big as a man" before he reached the land of
the Zunis. History does not record the fact.

Marcos de Niza followed closely behind the
black man. On a mesa he looked down upon the
village of Hawikuh. Where were the palaces?
Where was the gold? Here he learned of the
fate of the black man and dared not go on.
Would he dare to return to Mexico City and
reveal the truth? He erected a cross and took
possession of the land in the name of the King
of Spain.

Back in Mexico City the riches of the Seven
Cities of Cibola increased with every telling,
and Captain-general Francisco Vásquez de
Coronado was ready to lead the main expedition
to the fabulous land of gold and jewels. With
banners flying and trumpets blaring the conquistadors, three hundred strong, followed by a
thousand Indians and as many horses with great
herds of sheep and pigs bringing up the rear,
marched away with the blessings of the viceroy
and the prayers of the padres.

Across the deserts and mountain passes the
conquering Spaniards pressed on. When they
met Marcos de Niza, no one was in the mood to

strange black man. Four days after leaving the
two friars, the Moor sent a runner back with a
cross "as big as a man." De Niza did not question the Moor and assumed that he had, indeed,
found the treasure of the Seven Cities of Cibola.
He immediately sent the cross on to the viceroy
in Mexico City. Although his companion was
still unable to travel, De Niza left him behind
and pushed northward on the trail of Black
Stephen.

The Moor had reached the land of Cibola,
and there were seven villages, but instead of
jeweled palaces he found mud huts; instead of
gold in abundance, there was poverty and
misery; instead of friendly and curious Indians,
there was hostility. The Zunis of New Mexico
were not awed by the color of Estevanico's skin

accept the friar's true account of the villages of Cibola. What does a priest know of treasure? Let him stick to his beads! Forward!

The Zunis met the conquistadors head on, but they were no match for the well-armed Spanish soldiers. After a short fight the conquerors entered the land of Cibola. Coronado's rage at finding no treasure could not be contained. He ordered the slaughter of the Indians, somehow blaming them for possessing no wealth, and the poor Zunis were all but annihilated.

In September, Coronado's main army reached the village of Tigeaux, near the present town of Bernalillo, New Mexico, and set up winter headquarters. The Tigeaux Pueblos revolted against their uninvited visitors and were subjugated with such brutal severity as to incur Indian hostility to the Spaniards for the remainder of their stay in North America.

There was a turn of events in Tigeaux, however, that brought hope of yet discovering a land of great treasures. A plains Indian captive of the Pueblos, called El Turko (the Turk) by the Spaniards, told the conquerors of a fabulously rich country far to the east named Quivira. Coronado listened eagerly and got directions from El Turko for the way to this golden land. As soon as spring came, Coronado started eastward with his entire force.

After thirty-seven days of dreadful forced marching the food supply was almost exhausted and only buffalo meat was available. It was apparent that El Turko's directions were misleading—deliberately so, thought Coronado. The main army was sent back to Tigeaux, while a smaller party of thirty picked men headed north where new Indian guides said the true Quivira would be found.

Coronado urged his men on and finally they came to the land of the Quiviras (Wichita Indians) in eastern Kansas. Again there were no populous cities with streets of gold. The Quiviras didn't even know what gold was, much less possess it.

In early April of 1542, after a bitter winter of discouragement and disillusionment, Coronado and his army of treasure hunters started back to New Spain. His report to Mendoza in 1543 was a sad admission of failure. No gold had been found; there was no new wealth to be added to the Spanish Crown. No one yet knew that the vast new lands gained for Spain by the expedition were fabulously rich in minerals and would later yield millions in gold and silver.

The first treasure hunt in America—and the greatest—ended in abject failure, but the spirit of the conquistadors still lives in the hearts of men who climb the mountains and cross the deserts in search of modern treasure.

6.

THE SPANISH TREASURES OF THE SOUTHWEST

WHEN SPAIN was a world power her explorers ranged the earth in search of new lands and new riches. It was the Spanish who first tapped the vast riches of Peru, of Venezuela, of Mexico, and of the southwestern United States.

Wherever the Spanish explorer went he was seeking one thing—treasure, whether it was in the ground or already possessed. Wherever he found treasure, he took it over and directed it back to the mother country. This greed for treasure made Spain one of the most powerful and wealthy countries in the world during the early days of Spanish exploration in the New World.

The first Spanish explorations in the southwestern United States were the disappointing ventures of Marcos de Niza and Francisco Vásquez de Coronado, but those who followed in their footsteps found the treasures the earlier explorers had walked right over in their search for the fabled Seven Cities of Cibola.

A few of the Franciscan friars accompanying the Coronado expedition into the southwestern United States remained to take up their religious work among the half-civilized Indians of the new country. Later on they were joined by others, but the unappreciative Indians, with little taste for the white man's brand of religion, put most of them to death.

In 1582 a Spaniard named Antonio de Espejo was sent into Arizona and New Mexico to find out what was happening to the Franciscan padres who disappeared among the Indians. Espejo was instructed also to keep a sharp lookout for gold and silver. On the Bill Williams Fork, west of the present site of Prescott, Arizona, he found silver ore so close to the surface of the ground that it could be dug out by hand in big chunks.

Although very little is known of the early mining activities of the Spaniards in the Southwest, there are many stories about the gold and silver

verted Indians were employed virtually as slave laborers. When the ore was brought from the ground it was transported to either the *arrastres* located near the missions or the mines, ground into a fined powder, and smelted by the crude methods of the times. Many piles of slag from the old mission smelters have been located and occasionally have led to the discovery of the mine from which the slag was taken.

If the mine was located a considerable distance from the mission—and many were—a camp would be established near the mine entrance. Here the padres would build a small chapel

mines they worked before the coming of the Americans. Like the American prospector of later years, the Spanish miner was always looking for a richer strike, abandoning valuable finds to seek new locations. When he abandoned a mine he concealed it by covering it with stones or a large rock. Often he would carve a symbol on the covering rock so that he might again find the mine.

Few records of early Spanish mines are in existence, but traces of early mining activities are frequently uncovered and these have led to the rediscovery of some old Spanish mines. There are for sale in the Southwest many aged and crumbling maps purporting to be genuine that indicate the locations of rich ores. Beware of them. If they were of any value they would not be for sale.

The mission padres are known to have worked several rich mines in southern Arizona. Con-

where the spiritual needs of the Indians could be attended to. Above the entrance to the mine itself would be placed a wooden cross, or perhaps one would be carved in the rock there. Modern searchers for lost Spanish mines look for these signs.

Of the many stories of lost Spanish mines none is more intriguing than that of the famed Cave of Gold in Colorado—*La Caverna del Oro*. Rumors of the rich mine in the Sangre de Cristo Mountains southwest of Pueblo had persisted since white traders first came to the country, but the facts were vague.

One day in 1918 a United States Forest Ranger was visiting an aged Mexican woman in Santa Fe, New Mexico. The wrinkled old lady claimed to be one hundred and ten years old, and nobody could dispute the fact. She had lived a lot of history and she remembered well the old Spanish days in Sante Fe. As a child she had often visited a cave in the Sangre de Cristo Mountains which, she claimed, was the source of much Spanish gold. The miners had dug deep into the side of a mountain and there was *muy oro!*

"Where was the mine located?" asked the ranger. The old woman told him as best she could. "Go down 500 feet in the cave," directed the aged Mexican. "There you will find an oak door. Open the door and you will be in the mine shaft."

A year or so later, in the summer of 1920, the ranger was exploring on the eastern slope of Marble Mountain in the Sangre de Cristo range where he located a cave. The entrance was little more than a volcanic fissure, and the interior was dark and muddy from seeping water. Indistinguishable names were carved on the limestone walls. A broken and rusty shovel lay where someone had dropped it many years before. A length of rotting rope fell to pieces at his touch. Here, indeed, was evidence of some kind of early mining activity! Was it the Cave of Gold? The ranger, however, was not prepared to undertake further exploration at the time.

Several later expeditions to Marble Mountain failed to reach the 500-foot level because of the dangerous condition of the walls, but in 1932 a well-organized party made another try.

About 1000 feet below the entrance to the cave they found the remains of an old log and stone building, which they thought might have been a fort designed for the protection of the mine and its workers.

Slowly the explorers worked their way down to the 500-foot level where the oak door was supposed to lead to the mine shaft. There was no door. Scattered about, however, were the crumbled remains of more shovels, bits of rope,

a crude single-jack, and an ancient hammer thought to have been of Spanish make. Poking about in the shadows of their faint lights, the entrance to a shaft was eventually located. They followed this for a distance of 2500 feet without reaching its end, but the walls had caved in, making further progress impossible. No ore was found, nor has anyone since found the slightest trace of gold in Marble Cave. Yet, who dug the shaft so far into the mountain? Does it lead to the secret of the Cave of Gold?

Around the old cow town of Dodge City, Kansas, there is a story that Coronado buried treasure about four miles west of the city.
(There is every reason to believe that the Spanish explorer did reach this far north in his search for the Gran Quivira.) The story goes that when word was received that a large band of Indians was about to attack, the treasure carried for the pay of the soldiers was hurriedly buried and never reclaimed.

It has been more than a hundred years since a Spanish flag has fluttered over any part of the great Southwest, and now Spanish grandees are seen only in the movies, but the stories of Spanish treasure never die. Many old Mexicans whisper softly to the stranger of buried treasure and lost mines, but *Madre Diós, señor,* it is not belong to us!

7.

SPANISH GALLEONS AND THE TREASURE FLEETS

WHEN SPAIN WAS A GREAT WORLD POWER, her galleons were famed throughout the world. With colorfully painted sails and royal banners and pennants flying in the breeze, these proud ships roamed the seas of the world in search of treasure to carry home to the Spanish kings. They were the most famous ships of their time, but not the most seaworthy.

A typical galleon was perhaps 70 feet long at the keel with a distinctive high poop deck and a forward deck that might be as much as 90 feet above the water. This awkward design caused them to pitch and plunge in heavy seas and held down their speed so much that they were easy prey for pirates. The top speed for a galleon came near a mere 50 to 70 miles a day. Some of our modern ocean liners make half that speed in one hour!

After only four voyages to and from America a galleon was considered worn out and unfit for further duty. Her seams were opening under the constant strains of the seas, and her wooden hull was usually ravaged by boring insects. She was retired from service, that is, if she lived through four round-trip voyages.

The galleon was built to serve as a fighting ship as well as a cargo carrier. On each of the lower yardarms was placed a basket-shaped fighting top, often 40 to 50 feet in circumference. From these fighting tops crew gunners would fire muskets when the vessel was in battle action.

On the main and second decks, protruding from portholes, were the heavy guns designed to hold off any enemy vessel. Perhaps they could have done so if the galleons had possessed

29

sufficient speed and maneuverability to bring them into effective range. As it was, the galleon usually came out a poor second in combat.

The hull and superstructure of the galleon were emblazoned with gold, yellow, and flaming red carvings, while brightly colored coats of arms fluttered from every spar and mast. She was a beautiful ship, but her beauty offered little protection from the pirates!

lucky enough to be overtaken by a pirate craft.

Unseaworthy, slow and awkward, and manned by untrained seamen, it is little wonder that many a colorful galleon found her last resting place in Davy Jones's Locker or on the sands of a lonely beach, her treasure to rest there until found by a lucky treasure hunter or to be washed ashore a few coins at a time as the angry sea battered her breaking hulk to pieces.

Life aboard a galleon was rough and dangerous. Crewmen and gunners were herded together in small, bug-infested cabins reeking with the stench of bilge water. Food consisted of a small ration of salted meat or fish and a quart or less of fresh water daily. Often the crewman would gamble away his daily portion of food and go hungry until his luck changed or a friendly mate took pity on him. Scurvy was a common ailment, causing a man's teeth to fall out of his gums.

When two galleons met on the high seas, ceremonial salutes were exchanged until they were out of sight of each other. It was not uncommon for a galleon to waste her entire supply of powder and shot in this manner, and later be forced to surrender without firing a shot if un-

Each year two great Spanish fleets formed in the Caribbean Sea to transport the treasures of South America and Mexico to Spain. The first fleet was called the *Galleone* and consisted of the ships hauling the gold and silver from the mines of Peru. They would sail from the west coast of South America to Panama where the treasure would be unloaded and carried across the Isthmus of Panama on mules. Here it would be loaded on to other galleons and taken to Havana, Cuba.

The mines of Peru were incredibly rich, and their gold and silver bars would be supplemented with the riches stolen from the Incas. Other galleons would stream into Havana loaded with cargoes of gold from Venezuela and pearls from the island of Margarita.

The second fleet, called the *Flota* would sail from Vera Cruz, Mexico, loaded with gold and silver from the rich mines of Mexico. It, too, would sail for Havana, where all the galleons would be formed into one great fleet under the command of an admiral. When all the ships were ready to sail, the admiral would receive secret orders instructing him on the course to be sailed to Spain.

With a heavily armed convoy of *pataches*, smaller and swifter vessels than the galleons, the caravan would set sail on the 4000-mile voyage. Across the Caribbean Sea, through the Old Bahama Channel the galleons went, skirting the Bahamas and turning north along the coast of Florida. By this time there was little order left in the fleet as vessel after vessel, unable to keep the speed of the faster ships, fell behind or was blown off the course, while some were lost in the fog off the Bahama Banks. These stragglers became the prey of pirates watching for just such a lone vessel to waylay and rob.

Although pirates claimed a great toll of the Spanish galleons, the storms that sweep the eastern coast of Florida and the Gulf area from June through December were an even greater enemy. The exact number of vessels wrecked on the shores of Florida will never be known, of course, but they would amount to a good-sized fleet.

In October 1714 a fleet of fourteen galleons, all heavily loaded with treasure, was caught in a hurricane off the Florida keys. One vessel managed to ride out the storm and finally arrived in Spain with the bad news. The other thirteen ships piled up on the chain of islands extending from the mainland of Florida to Key West. It is not known how many millions of dollars' worth of treasure these vessels spewed on the beaches, but one vessel alone is said to have carried over three million pieces of eight in her hold. A salvage party recovered part of the treasure but other millions in silver and gold plate, in jewels and gems, rest there where the storm dumped them.

In the Gulf of Mexico storms frequently blew the ships of the *Flota* clear across the Gulf and onto the sandy shores of the Mustang and Padre islands off the coast of Texas. These long, slender islands are rich in stories of buried treasure and sunken ships, but the incessant battering of the sea has filled and washed away, built up and cut down with such regularity that the islands have probably moved several feet from their location during the days of the treasure galleons.

The treasure of the wrecked galleons meant little to the Indian natives of Florida and, except for some trinkets that they might pick up

to adorn their costumes, the vast piles of treasure were left undisturbed. An exception to this indifference was a chief of the Calusa tribe on the Florida west coast.

This wise old man had learned that treasure possessed a great bargaining value with the Spaniards. He accumulated a great pile of gold and silver bars which he buried near the Indian village somewhere along the shores of Charlotte Harbor. Soon the Spanish arrived and demanded the treasure. The chief offered to give up the treasure on one condition. The Spaniards were to take his sister and educate her to be a Christian. When she was returned to Christianize her people, the treasure would be surrendered.

The Spaniards were cool to the idea but finally submitted. The sister was taken to Havana and placed in a convent where she received the white man's education and was taught to be a lady. Then she fell in love with an influential Spanish official. They were married and left for Spain. The chief accused the Spanish of trickery and refused to give up the treasure. It is still searched for by hundreds of people every year.

Every once in a while the remains of an old galleon are found along Florida's shores, and more treasure has probably been recovered in Florida than will ever be known, but for every doubloon reclaimed, thousands still await a lucky finder. Florida is truly a treasure hunter's paradise.

8.

SUNKEN TREASURE SHIPS

IF YOU TOOK A CHART of the coastline of the United States and placed a cross at every spot along the shore where a ship has carried treasure to the bottom, you would have a map indicating the resting place of countless millions of dollars' worth of treasure.

Unlike most of the treasure buried under the ground, the actual location of many sunken treasure ships is known, and a great deal of treasure has been reclaimed from Davy Jones's Locker. The sea plays cruel tricks with the treasure seeker, however, and often grabs back its treasure just when success seems certain.

Treasure hunters actually had chains around the rotting bulk of the British frigate *DeBraak*, resting in about 14 fathoms of water a mile or so off Lewes, Delaware. There is an estimated $15,000,000 in her hold, including the jewels of Queen Marie Antoinette!

The *DeBraak* was one of the many English privateers preying upon the Spanish galleons. She had been very successful in her ventures and her hold was bulging with gold and silver bars, casks of doubloons, and box after box of precious stones and jewels.

With more than two hundred captured prisoners on board, the *DeBraak's* captain set sail for Halifax. While entering Lewes Harbor on May 15, 1798, a sudden squall broke across the bay and caught the *DeBraak* in a terrific swirl. She instantly overturned, filled with water, and sank in about 85 feet of water. Her entire crew as well as all of her ill-fated prisoners were lost.

Less than a year later a company of English salvages located the *DeBraak's* hull, but were twice driven away by sudden storms. The hulk finally shifted and the salvage attempt was abandoned.

A few years later the hull was again located and heroic efforts were made to bring up the treasure, but again the salvage expedition met with failure because of the strong winds and currents that prevail in the area of the wreck.

The *DeBraak* was all but forgotten until seventy-five years later when many ancient coins were washed ashore at Lewes after a particularly heavy storm. This renewed salvage interests, and several more attempts were made to reclaim the ship's fabulous treasure. All ended in failure, but right up to the present time the search for the treasure of the *DeBraak* goes on. One day the sea will yield its wealth to man's ingenuity.

Another sunken treasure ship whose exact location is known, but which has defied all efforts to recover its treasure is the *Merida,* which lies in about 55 feet of water some 50 miles or so off Cape Charles, Virginia.

The *Merida* was New York bound from Vera Cruz, Mexico. In her strong room were stored tons of gold and silver bars and coins, and perhaps also the crown jewels of Emperor Maximilian of Mexico. Off the Virginia cape, plowing through banks of heavy fog, the liner was rammed by the *Admiral Farragut* and immediately went to the bottom with all hands.

Several expeditions have sought the *Merida,* and one actually located her hull and succeeded in bringing up a single coin worth about seven dollars before shifting winds brought an end to the efforts. The remainder of the $5,000,000 aboard the *Merida* awaits a finder.

The wreckage of still another treasure ship rests right in the heart of New York City, passed daily by thousands of people in the world's largest city!

H. M. S. *Hussar* was a British pay ship carrying about $4,000,000 in gold and silver for the British soldiers stationed in New England. She was about to enter Hell Gate for the passage through to Long Island Sound when the vessel struck a submerged rock and swiftly went to the shallow bottom. In the hold were several American prisoners of war who went down with the treasure.

For many years the masts of the *Hussar* showed above the water, but strong currents and tides defeated all efforts of the English, and later of the Americans, to recover the treasure. In 1900 divers brought up an old iron anchor with the inscription "H. M. S. Hussar" cast in the metal, but after all these years and though knowing exactly where the hulk rested, salvagers have not been able to reclaim one cent of the *Hussar's* enormous treasure.

From Maine to Washington, around the entire coastline of the United States, these stories could be repeated a score of times by changing only the names of the ships and the details of their sinking. Even the reasonably warm and

shallow waters of the Great Lakes conceal the hulks of innumerable treasure vessels that have gone down in the violent and sudden storms characteristic of the area.

The coast of Florida and the Gulf of Mexico from Key West to Brazos Santiago, Texas, is studded with the rotting hulks of treasure ships. The treasures of some have been recovered, but there are still millions waiting under the sand and the mud of the ocean floor for the treasure hunter who can devise a method of recovering them.

The west coast of the United States, too, has its many sunken treasure ships. Along this coast sailed Spanish galleons from Manila to Mexico with the riches of the Orient. Many came to a final resting place along the rocky shores of Oregon and California. The gold from the mines of the Yukon and Alaska was carried out in ships to Seattle. The fogs and dangerous shores of western Canada claimed a heavy toll. They all wait to be reclaimed.

The first step, of course, in salvaging a sunken treasure ship is to locate the wrecked hull. Old records often indicate exactly where a ship was sunk, but this does not assure that the ship will be found where it went down. Under the surface waters of the sea, especially near shore, there is a constant battering of undercurrents, of shifting tides moving millions of tons of sand and silt as if swept before a broom. Today a

hulk may be washed free and exposed, but tomorow it may be buried under many feet of mud or sand.

When a hull is located by grappling hooks or other means, a diver is called in to determine the condition of the wreck. Has it fallen apart or is it intact? In what position does it lie? What equipment will be needed to bring the hull to the surface or to carry on salvage operations under the water? All these things are noted carefully.

In sinking, hulls often crack open, spilling bars of gold and silver and casks of coins across the ocean floor. When this happens, the work of the diver is multiplied many times because the tremendous forces of undercurrents and tides may wash the treasure far and wide.

Wooden hulls survive longer when buried in sand or mud than do the steel hulls of modern ships. Many wooden vessels have been brought to the surface not yet wholly decayed after hundreds of years in the water. Iron and steel will fall to pieces much more quickly.

Wooden ships are not nearly so likely to break up in sinking as metal vessels because, unless loaded with a heavy metal or mineral cargo, they will sink to the bottom at a relatively slow rate of speed, while an iron or steel ship will plunge downward like a rock. When the wooden ship hits bottom, especially in sand or mud, it is likely to remain intact, while a metal vessel will often crack open. This is an important point in salvaging a sunken ship because the condition of the hull will determine the difficulty of recovering the treasure.

A few feet below the surface of the ocean the forces of the waves are hardly felt, although there are enormous pressures from tides and undercurrents. Gradually the submerged wreck is covered with barnacles and marine growth, while the sediment of the sea slowly settles over it. If the tides and current are not too violent, a sandbar may be built up around the wrecked hull and remain for years until washed away by the heavy battering of a sudden storm.

When treasure that has remained under water for many, many years, is brought to the surface, it little resembles the bright and shiny metal we associate with gold and silver. It is so encrusted with hardened layers of dead marine growth as to be almost indistinguishable from a piece of rusted iron. A piece of metal once washed up on the coast of Florida was kicked around on the beach for weeks before a curious boy dragged it home and cleaned it up. It was a gold bar from a wrecked treasure galleon!

9.

PIRATES AND PIRATE TREASURE

As LONG AS there have been ships, there have been pirates, but the real growth of piracy occurred in the sixteenth century when it was actually encouraged by some nations, although thinly disguised as a war measure.

Suppose you were the owner of a small ship back in the 1700's and you sailed the seas under the flag of England. You roamed from port to port, picking up whatever cargo was available. Your risk was great and your return was small.

Your country went to war, we will say, with Spain. You were told that you could use your ship to attack any vessel flying the flag of Spain. You could seize its cargo, keep a reasonable share for yourself, and turn the remainder over to the Crown. As a protection you would be given an official-looking document called a "letter of marque." This was your license, or commission, to attack the ships of certain nations. It was all very legal.

This was an attractive offer and you, like many others, accepted it. Because you sailed in a privately owned vessel, you became known as a "privateer."

You armed your ship as best you could and hired a crew of rough, adventure-seeking men. You promised each a share of your loot. One day your ship was outfitted and you set sail in the shipping lanes from South America to Spain. You knew it was here that the rich Spain-bound galleons would be found.

Day after day, week after week, your little vessel plowed along, pitching and rolling in the boiling seas, all hands anxiously searching the horizon for a Spanish sail. One day you spotted your prey—a lone galleon strayed far from its course. Your ship was the faster and you finally overtook the treasure ship. You called your crew to battle stations.

Your signal to surrender was answered with a salvo from the galleon's gun decks. You replied immediately, and the battle was on. Shot whistled through your rigging, but your crew was well trained, calm, and accurate. Soon your faster vessel was in a position to fire a broadside. The treasure ship shook from stem to stern. Masts and sails crashed at the feet of the bewildered Spaniards. You came in closer and riddled the stricken vessel with a hail of musket fire.

You pressed the fight, moved in closer, and prepared to board the galleon for the finishing hand-to-hand fight. It was not necessary. The Spanish master signaled surrender, and a shout of victory went up from your crew.

Your men boarded the galleon and placed its crew in irons. A quick survey showed that the vessel was undamaged below the water line. All hands worked feverishly to put the ship in sailing condition. When this was completed, you headed with your captured prize for an isolated cove on a lonely shore.

Safely anchored alongside the captured vessel in protected waters, you set about to transfer the galleon's treasure to the hold of your own vessel. There were boxes of silver bars from Peru and gold from Mexico, sacks of gold and silver ornaments, jewelry and precious stones, casks of coins, each carefully stamped with the royal symbol of the Spanish Crown.

You estimated your share of the prize and found that you had cleared more money than you would have in several years of peaceful sailing. Your men were rich, too, and anxious to put to sea again. In the months that followed you were lucky and captured several more disabled vessels or ships that had strayed from their convoy. At last the hold of your ship was bursting with treasure and you sailed for England.

You kept only the share of treasure allowed you in your "letter of marque," but one day a rival captain—a privateer like yourself—accused you of keeping part of the King's share. You could not clear yourself and your license was revoked. Soon you were declared a pirate. It was the gallows if you were caught.

Hunted down now by the ships of your own country, you turned your guns upon any vessel you came across. You were, in fact, a real pirate, forced to hide in safe and lonely waters where other pirates like yourself sought refuge and safety. Before long you became a member of a pirate gang.

Your wealth became the envy of every man in your crew, and you had to be on constant guard to protect your treasure as well as your life. You were forced to rule with the cutlass and pistol for you were dealing with dangerous men.

As your wealth increased and filled the hold of your ship, you were forced to dispose of it. You sailed into a lonely inlet and carefully selected a spot to bury your treasure. You chose a few among your crew whom you thought could be trusted—you never could be sure—and sent the others inland to forage for supplies. When they were gone you took your treasure ashore and buried it.

If time permitted, you made a rough map of your treasure site, indicating permanant landmarks, the latitude and longitude, and any other information that would enable you to find the place again. Your treasure might be there when you returned, or it might not be. And perhaps you would never return—for yours was a dangerous life.

Some of your fellow pirates would alter the treasure-burying routine by killing all members of the crew who actually knew the burial place of the treasure. Their bodies would be dumped into the pit on top of the treasure. Pirates believed that anyone who might be digging for the treasure would be frightened away by the skeletons.

Another favorite trick used by pirates to conceal their secret was to maroon on a lonely island all the men who knew the treasure site. Here they would be left to any fate that overtook them—probably starvation.

This was the manner in which many pirates got their start—from honest seamen, to privateers, to piracy. By 1800 there were perhaps as many as two thousand pirates sailing the seven seas, burying their treasure in lonely spots all over the world. Captain Kidd, the famous pirate whose treasure is still sought in many places along the east coast of the United States, started his piratical career in exactly this manner. He ended it when he was captured in Boston and taken to England, where he was tried and hanged.

Pirates naturally banded together for mutual protection and congregated in areas where the greatest number of prizes were available. The Caribbean Sea was a rich hunting ground because of the great numbers of treasure-laden galleons sailing its waters. It became known to the pirates as the Spanish Main.

So many pirates gathered in the islands of the West Indies that an organization was formed to control and regulate their activities and to make laws. These laws were unique in some respects. First, they established the exact share each crew member was to receive from a captured prize. In case of an accident or injury in battle, the captain of the pirate vessel was compelled to pay the wounded man until he was able to work again. If an eye or a limb was lost, the injured man was paid a cash settlement!

At least one British governor in the West Indies actually protected the pirates in exchange for a share of their loot. Eventually the situation became so bad that the English dispatched a fleet to chase the pirates out of the Caribbean Sea.

The Caribbean pirates roamed far and wide, touching on many lonely shores, but the shores of Florida and the Gulf Coast were favorite haunts. Who knows how many buried treasure there?

10.
THE BURIED TREASURE OF CAPTAIN KIDD

OF ALL THE PIRATES who ever sailed the seven seas, Captain William Kidd is perhaps the most famous, as well as the most remarkable because there is some doubt as to whether he actually was a pirate! Some pirate historians assert that he was merely a bold and honest sea captain caught in a chain of fatal circumstances.

In the colonial days of New England there was little manufacturing in this country, and most of the goods had to be secured from overseas. This, of course, led to the development of a considerable merchant marine, and ships from New England roamed the seas of the world. Captain Kidd was the commander of one of these ships sailing out of New York.

Because England was habitually at war with France, Spain, and other countries, little protection was given the merchant ships, and piracy increased by leaps and bounds as pirates learned that the rich cargoes of the merchant ships were easy prey.

Finally, when conditions became so bad that no vessel was safe on the high seas, King William III of England called a meeting of some prominent gentlemen in London and presented an extraordinary plan for exterminating the pirates and getting rich at the same time! The plan called for the forming of a private company that would wage war on the pirates and capture their stolen cargoes. These treasures would be divided among the members of the King's company in proportion to the amount of money each put up to start the venture!

Among the several wealthy lords who jumped at the chance to enter into a private business venture with the king was Richard Coote, Earl of Bellomont. Furthermore, he knew just the man to command the privateers, a certain Captian Kidd from New York who happened to be in London at this very time. This man Kidd, Bellomont declared, was a seaman of tried courage and integrity, a "true and well-beloved" man of the sea.

Little did it matter that the King's clever plan was designed less to clear the seas of pirates than to fill his own empty coffers with loot pirated from the pirates; it was a sure thing and would get underway immediately.

Without delay Captain Kidd was summoned before the King. At first he showed little interest in the plan but, persuaded by Bellomont, he soon gave in and accepted a commission and a share in the King's company. He was a partner of the King's! Not bad for a sea captain!

In the galley *Adventure* carrying thirty guns and eighty men, Kidd sailed in March 1696 for New York. There he increased his crew to one hundred and fifty-five men, said goodbye to his wife and children, and sailed away for the pirate-infested Red Sea. During the summer of 1697 one third of that crew died of cholera, and the captain found it increasingly difficult to control those who still lived. They were treasure hungry and wished to attack the ships of any country as long as the prize was rich enough. When they were on the verge of mutiny, Kidd killed the leader, a gunner named Moore, a move in which he felt perfectly justified because the safety of his—and the King's—ship was in jeopardy.

In the winter of 1698 Kidd's galley captured a rich prize, the *Quedah Merchant* carrying a cargo of silks, silver plate, jewels, and gold coins. He transferred his crew to the captured ship and scuttled the *Adventure*.

Meanwhile in England, King William was in trouble. His political enemies had learned of the private venture and were protesting the use of the Great Seal of England in private enterprises smelling of piracy! Finally the King submitted to pressure and, to save his own neck, sacrificed that of Captain William Kidd by declaring him a pirate!

Stopping at some West Indian ports on his triumphant return to England, Kidd was amazed to learn that he was wanted for piracy. What had he done that was not granted to him by royal commission? There must be a mistake, Kidd told his friend, Henry Bolton, an English trader, but Bolton convinced the captain that he was in serious trouble.

Transferring his treasure from the *Quedah Merchant* to Bolton's lighter six-gun sloop *San Antonio*, Kidd sailed for Boston where Lord Bellomont was now in the King's service as governor. Perhaps the whole thing could be ironed out with Bellomont who, after all, was one of his backers and also a partner of the King's!

Sailing into Long Island Sound, Kidd anchored the *San Antonio* off Gardiner's Island at the northern end of Long Island in June 1699, one month short of three years since he had sailed away from New York to rid the seas of pirates! John Gardiner saw the sloop lying off the island and rowed out to investigate.

Kidd welcomed Gardiner aboard and explained that he was on his way to Boston to see Lord Bellomont. He asked Gardiner's permission to land two Negro boys and a girl. Gardiner figured that it would be useless to object and so agreed. A few hours later Kidd sent two bales of goods and a fourth Negro ashore.

On the following morning Kidd exchanged some muslin and silks with Gardiner for a barrel of cider and six sheep. Soon afterwards the sloop *San Antonio* fired a four-gun salute and sailed away, leaving John Gardiner wondering what in the world was going on!

Three days later the sloop returned to Gardiner's Island, and Kidd sent ashore a chest, a box of gold, a small bundle of gold and gold dust, two thirty-pound bags of silver, and four bales of goods. With Gardiner's knowledge the treasure was buried at Kidd's Hollow on the inshore side of the island, and the sloop again sailed away.

In the meantime Kidd had sent a messenger to Boston with instructions to find out what kind of a reception he could expect from Lord Bellomont. A letter arrived telling Kidd that Bellomont had promised full cooperation and had said: "On my word and on my honor I will perform nicely what I have promised." The promise was a pardon from the King.

Greatly relieved, Kidd sailed for Boston, but stopped on the way at the mouth of the Connecticut River to put two chests of treasure ashore on Clarke's Island. These were entrusted to his old friend "Whisking" Clarke and buried on the island, leaving Kidd with just enough money for his expenses while in Boston.

Kidd arrived in Boston and walked the streets freely like any ordinary man. At the end of the week, however, Governor Bellomont, his partner, had him thrown in jail. Later he sent him back to England, first depriving him of all documentary evidence that might assist him in freeing himself at trial.

In England Kidd was convicted of piracy and sentenced to hang. On Friday, May 23, 1701, still protesting his innocence, he was hung from the scaffolding at Wapping-on-Thames. The scaffolding and the rope broke, and the grim job was completed from the limb of a tree. His remains were later cut down and preserved with tar so that the public might see what happened to pirates!

In New England authorities soon confiscated all the treasure left on Gardiner's Island and also the two chests deposited with Whisking Clarke. According to the official inventory, it amounted to 1,123 ounces of gold and 2,353 ounces of silver—hardly the proceeds of a three-year piratical venture!

So the treasure hunters may be right, and Captain Kidd's real treasure may be buried anywhere from Nova Scotia to Florida!

It is impossible to name even a small portion of the places searched for Captain Kidd's fabulous treasure. Here is a record of enough of those from Maine to Florida to give you an idea of the really ubiquitous nature of the famed Kidd treasure.

MAINE

Codlead Marsh, where Codlead Creek empties into Penobscot Bay. Thousands have searched for Kidd's treasure here, and a few old coins have been found.

Deer Isle, Casco Bay. A great deal of searching has been done here for Kidd's treasure. Many years ago it was the scene of a treasure

hoax that caused a lot of excitement, when an unscrupulous person claimed to have found Captain Kidd's treasure chest.

Musselridge Channel near Twobush Island. Many efforts have been made to find Kidd's treasure in this vicinity and the story persists that this was the burial spot.

Richmond's Island near Old Orchard Beach. In 1855 a farmer plowed up a ring and old coins all pre-dating Captain Kidd's time, and the incident led to the belief that Kidd's treasure was still to be found in this area.

Fort Point Cove where Stony Brook empties into the Penobscot River. Hundreds of people have dug here for the four chests of treasure said to have been brought ashore by Kidd and four slaves.

Money Cove on Isle au Haut. This is another traditional digging place for Kidd's treasure. None has been found.

Monhegan Island. Captain Kidd has been the cause of much digging on the island, but as far as is known, nothing has been found.

Squirrel Island, Boothbay Harbor. On the east coast of Squirrel Island is Kidd's Cave penetrating 150 to 200 feet into solid rock and so named because it was thought to be the hiding place of Kidd's treasure.

Money Holes near Dresden Mills. The Money Holes are the result of thousands of tons of earth being dug up in search of Kidd's treasure. One pit went down to a depth of 80 feet!

Edgecomb. A local story says that Samuel Trask, one of Kidd's lieutenants, was delegated to bury part of Kidd's treasure and did so on his farm near here.

Banks of the Penobscot River between Prospect and Frankfort. This is another of the many Maine coast sites where there has been a great deal of digging for Kidd's treasure.

Jewell's Island, Casco Bay. A Nova Scotian came to the island around 1900 with a map claiming to show where Kidd's treasure was buried. He took an old sea captain into his confidence and the two were seen to go up the beach together. The Nova Scotian was never seen again, but people later found a great hole dug on the southeast shore, and it looked as if a large chest had been taken from it. Years later the skeleton of a man was found in the crevice of a rock covered with stones. Was it the Nova Scotian?

Sheepscot River. A chest of Kidd's treasure was supposedly dropped in the river. Many years later when the anchor of a sloop was

being raised it brought up a chest caught in a fluke. It dropped back into the river, however, and was never found again.

Sheepscot River above Wiscasset. This is another spot where Kidd's treasure has been searched for many times.

Outer Heron Island, Boothbay Harbor. Just before 1900 two men came to the island with a treasure map and searched the area for a month. At one spot they dug down 30 feet and uncovered old oak planks, but no treasure.

VERMONT

Bellows Falls. The finding in 1839 of two Spanish silver dollars of a very early date by some workmen digging a canal immediately touched off a search for Captain Kidd's treasure.

NEW HAMPSHIRE

Antrim, Hillsboro County. Kidd is said to have buried treasure on the shores of Rye Pond near the town of Antrim, and many searches have been made for it in the boggy soil near the pond.

MASSACHUSETTS

Tarpaulin Cove on Naushon Island. The cove on the east shore of the island was said to have been the last port of call for Captain Kidd before his arrest in Boston, and many people think that his treasure was buried here.

Devil's Den near Wilmington, Middlesex County. Many years ago a stranger and a Negro were seen to approach the small cave in a loaded wagon. In the afternoon the wagon returned empty and without the Negro. It was supposed that the wagon contained part of Captain Kidd's treasure and that the Negro was killed to guard the secret.

Cheshire, Berkshire County. There is a local story that Kidd came to Cheshire and buried a chest of gold before setting out on a pirating adventure. The story has never been proved— nor disproved.

Plum Island. The older residents of Plum Island tell of many searches made for Captain Kidd's treasure supposedly buried on a certain low hill on the island.

Turners Falls on the Connecticut River, Franklin County. On Captain Kidd's Island near here the famous privateer is said to have buried an iron chest full of gold and jewels, and for generations treasure seekers have dug up the island from end to end.

Hog Island, Essex County. A story has long persisted that Kidd buried a chest of gold on Hog Island, and many treasure hunts have been made for it.

Conant's Island, Boston Bay. Before entering Boston on his last voyage Kidd is said to have stopped at Conant's Island and buried the greater part of his treasure.

Winthrop Beach, Boston Bay. Captain Kidd is said to have landed at Winthrop Beach in 1699, and ever since the news of his hanging in England people have dug in the vicinity of the old John Allen farm for the treasure they say he must have buried there.

RHODE ISLAND

Block Island. Long believed to be the hiding place of Kidd's treasure, the surface of the island has been dug over by treasure seekers, and it is thought that some booty has been found.

Conanicut Island. Kidd is known to have visited the island and is believed to have left treasure in the care of an old pirate named Tom Paine. Pirate's Cave (hard to find), a hole in the rocks, is the popular place to search for Kidd's gold.

CONNECTICUT

Clarke's Island in the Connecticut River. It is here that Kidd visited his friend Whisking Clarke on his last journey to Boston and supposedly left two treasure chests which were buried. Whether or not the chests were later discovered is a matter in dispute.

Money Island in the Thimbles group. Money Island is one of many small islands off Stony Brook. Here Kidd is said to have buried his treasure "in the fissures of a large rock formation connected with the island but under water at high tide."

Thimble Island in the Thimbles group. In 1924 a curious old gold ring was found on the island by a New Haven fireman. It was believed that the ring was part of the treasure buried by Kidd on the island.

Stratford Point, Fairfield County. When Captain Kidd cruised up Long Island Sound in 1699 it is said that he came ashore on Stratford Point and buried a heavy chest in the sand. A Negro boy walking along the beach is supposed to have witnessed the act but was afraid to tell anyone what he had seen until years later.

Old Lyme, New London County. There is a local story that Captain Kidd buried a chest of gold under a boulder near here.

Wethersfield, Hartford County. There is a story in this area that Kidd sailed up the Connecticut River to a point near by known then as Tyron's Landing. After burying his treasure he is said to have killed one of his men with a water bucket.

NEW YORK

Rye Beach. A story common in this vicinity is that of a stranger who begged a farmer's wife for shelter on a stormy night and in the morning filled her apron with gold pieces. Ever since, people have dug the beach searching for Kidd's treasure.

Hudson Highlands in the vicinity of West Point. The story persists that Kidd's ship, the *Quedah Merchant*, was sailed up the Hudson to the Highlands and scuttled after Kidd had exchanged the ship for the sloop *San Antonio*. A vast amount of plunder is said to be buried near by.

Peekskill. Kidd is said to have hidden his treasure near here.

Sleepy Hollow. A search was made here for the pirate chest of Captain Kidd when the skeleton of a Negro was found many years ago. There had long been a story that the privateer buried treasure here and killed the Negro slave who assisted him.

Grassy Point on the Hudson River. This is another point along the Hudson to which stories of Kidd's buried treasure have brought many treasure hunters.

Captain Kidd's Cave on the Hudson River. High on the face of Crow's Nest is the cave in which Kidd is said to have buried one of his treasure chests when on a visit up the Hudson in 1699.

Kidd's Point on the Hudson River. At the base of Dunderberg, the narrowest place in the navigable Hudson, is Kidd's Point where the privateer is supposed to have lived for a while and to have buried his treasure.

Money Hill, Westchester County. There has long been a story around Croton that Kidd buried his treasure on Money Hill near here. Pieces of eight and other old coins have been found in the neighborhood.

Conesville, Schoharie County. Not far from Conesville, on a small knoll between two ancient trees, many searches have been made for Kidd's treasure, said to have been buried there by an old Indian.

Fishers Island at northern end of Long Island Sound. On this long narrow island Captain Kidd is said to have buried two chests of gold before sailing on his last voyage. Years ago there was much digging for it but, as far as is known, nothing was found.

NEW JERSEY

Cape May. Captain Kidd is said to have sailed in to Cape May Point and, after filling his casks with fresh water, buried his treasure and sailed away.

Cliffwood Beach, Monmouth County. A local story in Cliffwood has it that Kidd buried a treasure chest on the beach near here, but the shoreline of Kidd's time is now far out to sea, thwarting search for the treasure.

DELAWARE

Bombay Hook Island. According to local stories this lonely and windswept island was selected by Captain Kidd as a cache for his treasure, and much unsuccessful digging has been done for it.

Kelly Island. James Gillan, a member of Captain Kidd's pirate crew, is said to have buried part of the Kidd treasure on Kelly Island between two trees close to a large boulder. Although many people have searched for it, no one has ever found it.

GULF OF MEXICO

11.

THE BURIED TREASURE OF JEAN LAFITTE

FOR MORE THAN A HUNDRED YEARS the El Dorado of the Gulf Coast has been the treasure of Jean Lafitte which is reportedly buried in a hundred different places from the Florida Keys to the southern tip of Texas. When someone comes into sudden and unexplainable wealth in Louisiana, it is common to hear said of him: "Ah, so he found Lafitte treasure, eh?"

Jean Lafitte, who liked to be known as a gentleman, was born, lived, and died a mystery. He came to New Orleans about 1804 as "Captain Lafitte" of the French privateer *La Soeur Chérie,* which dropped anchor for repairs and provisions. Five years later he and his brother Pierre were owners of a blacksmith shop which was used as a warehouse for the disposal of smuggled goods.

Over on Barataria, now known as Grand Terre or Grand Isle, a motley collection of men from many nations made their headquarters and raided the ships sailing the Gulf. They needed a market for their stolen goods, and Jean Lafitte was just the type of man they were looking for. He moved in the best circles in New Orleans and was known as a shrewd business man. The pirates of Barataria used him as their business agent and banker.

By 1811 Jean Lafitte had grown wealthy and one by one he took over the independent little pirates who supplied him with stolen loot. Soon he was in complete command and the pirates found themselves taking orders from "the boss." He organized the pirates and directed the operations of about half a dozen ships sailing under the flag of the infant Republic of Cartagena, now part of the Republic of Colombia.

In direct violation of United States revenue laws, the spoils of piracy were smuggled into New Orleans and sold to merchants and planters. It was difficult for the authorities to stop these activities because the merchants of New Orleans wanted the cheap merchandise and also the United States government was very unpopular at the time. Lafitte moved about like a prince with little fear of being molested by the law, although several small expeditions were sent against him prior to the War of 1812.

During the struggle between England and the United States for control of the Mississippi, the British approached Lafitte and offered him for his services immunity for his past offenses and a captaincy in the British navy, as well as other rewards. Lafitte feigned acceptance and gained as much information as possible concerning the British plans to attack New Orleans. He promptly took this information to the Americans and offered the services of his pirates in the defense of New Orleans—all for a fancy price, of course. The Americans turned him down and sent a gunboat to destroy the pirate headquarters on Barataria.

Later, the offer to the American officials was made a second time, and General Andrew Jackson accepted. In the Battle of New Orleans the pirates acquitted themselves bravely and contributed to the defeat of the English. For their help President Madison issued full pardons for their past crimes with the understanding that the pirates were to abandon their stronghold on Barataria and cease all piratical activities.

For a time it appears that Lafitte tried to reform, but eventually he renewed his smuggling and again turned his band of pirates loose to prey upon ships of all flags. This was more than the authorities could stand, and a strong expedition drove him away from Barataria and all of Louisiana. Undismayed, Lafitte simply moved bag and baggage to Texas and settled down on what we now know as Galveston Island but which he named Campeachy.

Campeachy attracted pirates, soldiers of fortune, privateers, and adventurers from all over the world, including some four hundred officers and men from Napoleon's defeated armies. From his combination fortress, warehouse, and home known as Maison Rouge, Lafitte ruled with a smoking pistol and lived in the elegant manner of a lord.

During his occupancy of Galveston Island, Lafitte's ships never hesitated to attack any vessels thought to contain rich prizes, including more than one hundred Spanish ships. It was during this time that his immense fortune was accumulated. Together with what he had brought from New Orleans, it is thought that he had a personal treasure of more than $10,000,000!

Repeated attacks against ships of the United States brought an American warship to Galveston one day in 1820. Lafitte tried to reason with the authorities and promised that his men would respect the flag of the United States or be killed by his own hands. The United States Navy had had enough of Lafitte's promises, however, and he was ordered to leave Galveston.

His treasures were accumulated and loaded aboard ship. His pirate band was left on the island to shift for themselves, and Jean Lafitte sailed away. What happened to his treasure? That is a question that has never been fully answered, but you can be sure that it was buried at the earliest possible moment, at one or more spots, perhaps along the coast of Texas in the vicinity of Corpus Christi.

One of the most persistent stories concerning the site of his buried treasure seems to have some basis for credence. While engaged in pirate activities around the sandy islands off Corpus Christi, Lafitte's ship, the *Pride,* encountered a United States gunboat. Lafitte sailed up the Lavaca River with the warship in pursuit. The *Pride* hit a sandbar and Lafitte ordered the treasure taken ashore and the vessel scuttled. On the way across the salty marshes, Lafitte had a hole dug and the treasure buried in it. He took a compass reading of the exact spot and drove his Jacob's staff, a brass rod used by surveyors,

into the soft ground exactly above the treasure, until only the top of the rod was visible.

A San Antonio man named J. C. Wise, armed with definite clues obtained from two of the treasure bearers, made repeated searches along the marshy banks of the Lavaca River for the brass rod marking the treasure site. He was never able to find it.

Years later a rancher named Hill purchased the property near the mouth of the Lavaca and pastured his horses on the swampy bottom grasses. A Negro boy hired to herd the horses rode through the meadows one day looking for a stone or stump to tie his horse to while he took a nap. He stumbled on a brass rod sticking out of the ground, and after he had completed his rest he pulled the rod from the ground and took it to the ranch house with him that night.

It was several days before the rancher saw the rod lying around the corral and in the meantime it had rained hard. Recalling that Lafitte was supposed to have marked the site of his buried treasure with a similar instrument, he asked the boy about the rod. With all the help the boy could furnish, the marshes were thoroughly searched for the matted grass that would indicate the spot where he had rested. The lapse of time and the recent rains had destroyed all evidence, and the treasure chests of Jean Lafitte are still to be recovered at the mouth of the Lavaca River.

This is perhaps the most authentic Lafitte treasure site, but by no means the only one. Contraband Bayou, south of Lake Charles, Louisiana, has been searched many times for Lafitte's treasure, and a local story has it that the pirate once built a two-room log hut near the famous Barbé House which still stands at 2709 Shell Beach Drive. The remains of embankments thrown up by the pirates, behind which stood mounted guns, are still to be seen in Lake Charles, and it is claimed that Lafitte sank a schooner containing part of his treasure in the lake one dark night when pursuers were thought to be near.

Other Louisiana stories cite Jefferson Island as the burial place of Lafitte's treasure. Jefferson

Island isn't an island at all, but a salt dome rising from the flat prairie and resembling a tremendous mound. In 1923 a Negro employee called "Daynite" uncovered a quantity of Mexican gold and silver coins while digging for a culvert on Jefferson Island. Since for several years previously old coins bearing a 1754 date had frequently found their way into circulation in the area, it was concluded that part of Lafitte's treasure had been found at Jefferson Island.

At the height of his career Lafitte often visited d'Estrehan House up the river from New Orleans. The d'Estrehans were influential planters and on very friendly terms with the pirate

of Louisiana. According to local legend Lafitte once sailed a ship up the mouth of the Amite and buried a load of gold on the shore opposite Galvez Town.

From time to time hunts are made for Lafitte treasure at Pecan Island which, like Jefferson Island, isn't an island at all but a long oak-covered ridge rising abruptly from the surrounding country. When discovered about one hundred years ago, Pecan Island was completely covered with pecan trees and the ground was literally covered with human bones. No explanation of the bones has yet been found, but one theory is that this was the spot where Lafitte had his victims murdered. Treasure

chief. Local stories say that Lafitte took advantage of their hospitality to bury treasure on their property. Among the slaves who knew the story, it was commonly thought that the pirate returned to the house on stormy nights and pointed a bony finger at the hearth.

Between New Orleans and Baton Rouge, at the mouth of the Amite River, is the little village of Galvez Town which was an important shipping center during the Spanish domination

hunters have thoroughly dug up the island and in 1925, not content with digging, they used dynamite and almost blew the place to pieces. Not one old coin was uncovered for the trouble!

The shores of Lake Borgne in Louisiana have come in for a lot of treasure hunting by those who insist that Jean Lafitte buried part of his treasure before sailing away from Galvez Town. Others claim that the gentleman pirate visited Caillou Island west of Bayou Lafourche and deposited part of his treasure in the ground for safekeeping. There is some reason for suspecting that this is more than a theory, for $20,000 in old Spanish and Mexican coins was found on Caillou several years ago.

Working east around the Gulf Coast, you come to Fort Morgan (old Fort Bower), Alabama, on the tip of a long sandy peninsula separating Bon Secours Bay from the Gulf of Mexico, about thirty-three miles south of Mobile, Alabama. Many pirates operated in this area, including Jean Lafitte who is said to have buried treasure near the old fort. My efforts to search the area have repeatedly bogged down in Army, Navy and Coast Guard correspondence, all of whom have had a hand in the jurisdiction of the old fort.

Bayou Labatre is a small community of winding streets and small cottages amid tropical vegetation several miles south of Mobile. Lafitte and his pirate crew often sailed into the bayou and anchored under the safety of their shore guns while the crew went to Mobile to spend their gold. The pirate is said to have buried treasure near here on several occasions but the natives were afraid to search for it. So greatly was he feared that the more pious residents of the area sprinkled holy water in the doorways of their houses to keep him out. Children of later generations were told that Lafitte could reach out of the sea and pull them into the water if they were out too late at night!

There is scarcely an island along the vast Texas coast that does not have its favorite tale of buried Lafitte treasure. In 1889 some old Spanish coins and a large chest were found at Virginia Point near Galveston. The chest was empty but its proximity to the site of Lafitte's old Galveston headquarters led to the belief that someone had found part of the pirate's treasure.

In 1940 there was considerable excitement in the town of Anhuac near Galveston when Texas State authorities were asked for permission to salvage a strange ship that could be seen in the glittering sands of a small Galveston Harbor inlet. Several years previously some Spanish coins dated 1803 had been found on a near-by beach, which now helped substantiate the story that the vessel was one of Lafitte's treasure vessels. The State failed to grant salvage rights, however, and the treasure hunters have been frustrated to this day.

Lafitte's crews used Aransas Pass and many other points around Corpus Christi as hideouts. Here they would secure fresh water and provisions and divide their spoils. It is believed that the pirates buried three chests of treasure on Liveoak Point near Aransas Pass, and many searches are still made in the vicinity.

Sabine Pass was a thriving Texas town when Lafitte's men roamed the Gulf, and the pirate ships frequently sailed through the near-by waters or anchored close in. It is a treeless expanse of tall salt grass and just the kind of a place associated with buried treasure and pirate chests. There has been much digging here and several old coins have been found.

One could go on almost indefinitely enumerating the sites of Lafitte's buried millions. Of one thing there can be no question—he had treasure, immense quantities of it, and he secreted it in the ground at almost any spot from Florida to Mexico! You may take your choice!

What happened to this strange man? Presumably he passed his last years in piracy along the Yucatan coast, dying there of fever in 1826, although like his birth and most of his life, his end is surrounded in mystery and legend. But legend or no legend, as long as the lure of buried treasure endures, Jean Lafitte will forever inspire treasure hunters to dig deeper!

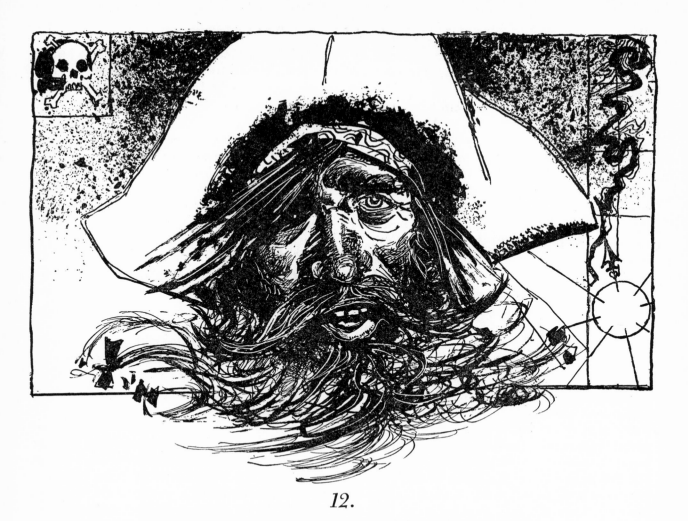

12.

BLACKBEARD'S BURIED TREASURE

IF JEAN LAFITTE WAS THE GENTLEMAN OF THE pirates, and William Kidd the honest seaman trapped by circumstance, then William Teach, better known as Blackbeard, was the most ferocious of the pirates—a ruthless, roaring demon who would sooner slit a throat than eat.

William Teach, even in his 'teens, was sailing the high seas in a pirate vessel commanded by Benjamin Thornigold, and it was from this master that young Teach received his first lessons in the use of terror. Thornigold was a qualified instructor, and young Teach an apt student.

William Teach even wanted to look like a pirate—a murderous villain whose very appearance would strike fear into the hearts of his victims. To accomplish this he grew the fullest, blackest, dirtiest beard a man ever wore. It

covered his face from hairline to neck, from ear to ear, and except for the narrow slits for his eyes, nose, and mouth, his entire head was a mass of twisted black hair.

After sailing the Spanish Main for several years with Thornigold, Teach acquired two vessels and struck out on his own. In the *Queen Anne's Revenge*, a French merchant ship captured in 1717, he scoured the seas with bloodthirsty madness, carving out a career for himself seldom equaled for sheer wantonness in all the history of piracy. In all the ships he captured there was only one fate for their crews—death. It might be by the pistol, the cutlass, or perhaps walking the plank, but if you fell into William Teach's hands you were certain to die by one means or the other!

51

Teach's favorite hangout was Ocracoke Island, North Carolina. His shallow vessels could evade the British warships by crossing through Ocracoke Inlet into Pamlico Sound. Here he could lie in safety while the English cooled their heels outside the bar, and he was in friendly waters because he had met Governor Charles Eden and had showered him generously with stolen booty.

Even among his own men Teach was a murderous tyrant, and although his stolen treasures amounted to millions he shared them with as few as possible. This is how he evaded a division of the spoils upon one occasion. There were four ships in his fleet, manned by about four hundred crewmen. Under the pretext of repairing and cleaning his vessels, he had all the treasure transferred to one ship. With about three hundred and sixty men on the other three ships, he ordered them beached on a lonely island off the North Carolina coast. (Beaching was the usual method of cleaning the hulls of ships in the old days.)

After disabling the three stranded vessels, Teach sailed away, marooning three hundred and sixty men and reducing his crew to forty. But even forty men was more than Teach wanted to share his gold and silver with. Figuring that he could man his lone treasure ship with twenty-three men, he promptly sailed to another isolated spot and sent seventeen men ashore to look for a suitable spot to cache the treasure. When they were out of sight, he again sailed away!

Teach had twelve or thirteen wives on Ocracoke, whom he dispensed with whenever they aroused his displeasure. Finally he took a fourteenth wife, and she persuaded Teach to give up piracy. He called upon his old friend Governor Eden and secured a full pardon for his crimes. Then, abandoning the Ocracoke colony, he and his bride sailed away to the Isle of Shoals off the New Hampshire coast.

Supposedly Teach buried a great deal of treasure on the Isle of Shoals during the few weeks that he spent there, but he had no more than finished the job than a British warship appeared. Leaving his new wife to get along as best she could, the pirate sailed away just in time to avoid capture. The quiet life of a retired and reformed pirate didn't appeal to him anyway, so he returned to Ocracoke and continued his bloodthirsty career.

In 1718 the Colonial government finally decided that Teach must be driven from the seas, and a young British captain, Robert Maynard, was given the job. His instructions were to bring in the pirate, dead or alive. If he was dead, it would save a hanging. But Teach had a pardon from a Colonial governor! That was all right, said Governor Spotswood of Virginia, bring the scoundrel in and there's a hundred pound reward for the act!

Maynard knew that he was dealing with a madman who would fight to the finish. First, he selected two vessels that could cross the shoals through Ocracoke Inlet. Then he hand-picked his crews. When all was ready he put to sea with a vow that he would not return without the pirate's head.

As Maynard's ship slipped through the shallow inlet and rounded the tip of the island, he glimpsed the spars of the pirate's vessel in the distance. At the same moment Teach saw the approach of the strange vessels and ordered his craft stripped for action. It was late in the evening and, before the British warships could be brought in close enough to open fire, darkness was upon them. Maynard decided to wait until morning.

At dawn the British ships moved in, and Blackbeard fired the first shot. Maynard replied by hoisting the King's colors. Because the British ships had been stripped of their heavy guns in order to lighten the vessels for the passage through the inlet, Blackbeard had the advantage in guns. Maynard figured that his faster vessels would even the odds, but one of his ships struck a bar and grounded. The situation was desperate now, but Captain Maynard continued to bear down on the pirate with all the sail he could pour on.

Seeing that he was to engage only one ship, Blackbeard waited until the vessel was almost upon him. Then he gave the command to fire a broadside. The British ship shook and shuddered, and a tangled mass of rigging crashed to the deck. When the smoke cleared, twenty-nine of Maynard's crew were dead or out of action with wounds. This left him twelve men including himself. Keeping the man at the helm and two others, Maynard sent the remaining eight below to wait his orders. Then he permitted the pirate vessel to come alongside.

Approaching the stricken vessel, Blackbeard picked out the four men on deck and concluded that the others were all dead. He roared the command to board the warship and, armed with two pistols and an enormous cutlass, he led his fourteen pirates onto the British ship. Maynard gave the signal and eight British seamen leaped from the hold, firing as they came.

The two captains made a wild dash for each other and fired at the same moment. One of Blackbeard's pistols misfired; his other shot was wild. Maynard's bullet caught the pirate in the leg, but Teach drew his cutlass and swung wildly for Maynard's head. The British captain drew his sword, and the two men

closed in on each other. A terrific blow from the pirate caught Maynard's sword and snapped it off at the hilt. The roaring and raging Teach raised his cutlass and prepared to swing at his disarmed opponent's head, but at that moment a British marine jumped upon the pirate chief and stabbed him in the neck.

Screaming like a mortally wounded animal, the pirate turned upon the marine, but by this time he was surrounded on all sides. Bleeding from twenty different wounds, the raving pirate fought on like a fanatic, remaining on his unsteady feet. Suddenly he tottered and dropped dead!

Captain Maynard finished his job and delivered the head of William Teach, beard and all, to the proper authorities. Fourteen of the pirates were hanged, and the notorious career of Blackbeard was ended.

What really happened to the fabulous Blackbeard treasure? On the evening before Captain Maynard forced the pirate's last bloody battle, one of Blackbeard's lieutenants suggested that it might be well for the pirate chief to tell someone where the treasure was hidden—just in case. Blackbeard replied: "Nobody but the Devil and me know where the treasure is, and the longer liver of us two shall have it all!"

Like Kidd's buried treasure, Blackbeard's is reported to lie in a hundred different places from Maine to Trinidad, including many spots along the east coast of the United States. Here are a few of them.

Isle of Shoals. This small group of islands about ten miles off the New Hampshire coast belongs partly to Maine and partly to New Hampshire. There are eight islands when the tide is low, six when it is high. Swept by every wind that blows and beaten by the seas, the islands are barren and bleak, the whole group indented with tiny coves and fringed with weeds and thistles.

Among the pirates who frequented the islands was William Teach who stayed on Smuttynose or Londoner for a few weeks and is supposed to have buried a large quantity of silver bars and pieces of eight. Samuel Haley, after whom Haley's Island is named, was engaged in building a fence on Smuttynose when he turned over a large stone and uncovered four silver bars. This was about 1880, and countless searches have been made since that date.

Burlington, New Jersey. According to a local story Blackbeard buried a chest of treasure near here under the foot of a large black walnut tree. On top of the chest he is said to have placed a dead Spaniard. In 1926 an effort was made to find the treasure, and excitement was high when diggers found old bones at the base of a walnut tree. They turned out to be the bones of a cow and Blackbeard's treasure is still unfound.

Blackbird, Delaware. Blackbird is a small hamlet supposedly named after Blackbeard who is said to have used Blackbird Creek as a harbor and to have buried treasure along its banks.

Blackbeard's Island, Georgia. Located in Sapelo Sound and adjoining Sapelo Island, this small heavily wooded island has been the scene of many searches for Blackbeard's buried treasure. An old fort made of "tabby" (a mixture of oyster shells and lime) and a tunnel leading from the fort to the sea are believed to have been built by the pirate.

Ossabaw Island, Georgia. Local stories claim that Blackbeard came to Ossabaw Island about 1715 and buried part of his loot.

Elizabeth City, North Carolina. On the south bank of the Pasquotank River, about three miles north of Elizabeth City, still stands an old brick house supposedly used by Blackbeard. At the doorstep for many years rested a large circular stone bearing the inscription: "E. T. 1709." On either side of the fireplace were closets communicating with a concealed passage leading from the basement to the river. The pirate is said to have buried a large quantity of treasure near the old house.

Plum Point, North Carolina. Plum Point is a narrow stretch of land in Beaufort County where Bath Creek flows into the Pamlico River. For more than two hundred years the story of a treasure chest buried here by Blackbeard has persisted and the ground has been dug over many times. In 1928 two men came across a large pit out of which a great number of bricks had been taken a short time previously. The bricks had formed an underground vault, and inside the remains of the vault were the clear marks of an iron chest. Old lumber around the pit indicated that a tripod had been erected so that the chest could be lifted out with a tackle.

Teach's Hole, Ocracoke Island, North Carolina. At the southern tip of Ocracoke Island is the small cove that served as Blackbeard's hideout for many years, and it was near here that he was killed. Almost every square foot of the sandy island has been turned over in the search for the large treasure believed to have been buried here by the pirate. According to local stories, a house in the village of Ocracoke was his home and the burial place of his treasure.

Amelia Island, Florida. Long thought to be the hiding place of Blackbeard's treasure, Amelia Island has been dug over persistently and a few gold doubloons were found in the mid-1930's.

Boca Raton, Florida. This is a small inlet a few miles south of Delray Beach on the Florida east coast. Old records indicate that several pirates took advantage of the inlet to escape pursuing warships, and one of these is said to have been Blackbeard.

13.

THE BURIED TREASURE OF BILLY BOWLEGS

IF IT IS TRUE that pirates don't live to a ripe old age, then Billy Bowlegs was certainly an exception. When he died in 1888 he had just rounded out ninety-three years.

Like the traditional pirate, Billy Bowlegs was a real scoundrel, but he had one unusual trait for a man of his profession. He hoarded his blood-stained treasure to his dying day. Although he possessed millions and could have lived out his later days like a king, he preferred his shack among the mangrove trees.

Whether or not William Rogers was his real name, it was the one he was using when he appeared in New Orleans about 1810 and acquired a plantation some seventy-five miles from the city. Here he married a Choctaw Indian woman and settled down to what appeared to be a respectable life. In due time the Choctaw bore him six children—four boys and two girls.

About the only thing known of Rogers' past was his English nationality, for he never talked. He had money when he came to New Orleans, but where he got it he kept to himself.

Soon tiring of plantation life, he moved into New Orleans where Jean and Pierre Lafitte held a monopoly on smuggling and piracy. Rogers became a member of the gang and about this time acquired the name of Billy Bowlegs.

Presumably Billy Bowlegs was one of Lafitte's Barataria pirates who took part in the Battle of New Orleans and so won pardons from the government. Later when Lafitte was forced to withdraw from the New Orleans area and removed bag and baggage to Galveston, Billy Bowlegs remained in New Orleans and acquired three small vessels. When his ships were equipped and ready to sail, he recruited a crew from Lafitte's old hands and moved up the Gulf to Santa Rosa Sound near Pensacola, Florida. Here he started a career of smuggling and piracy that was to make him a rich man.

No one will ever know how many ships Billy Bowlegs captured, nor how much loot he actually seized, but his name was feared up and down the coast. His particular prey were the Spanish treasure galleons plying the Gulf and he didn't have to capture many of these to accumulate a great fortune.

Realizing perhaps that the days of open piracy were rapidly coming to an end, Billy dis-

banded his crew in 1838 and set out to hide his treasure. On the north side of a small sandy island in Santa Rosa Sound he buried the bulk of his fortune which was in gold and silver ingots from the mines of Peru and Mexico. At another spot, on the mainland near by, he cached the minted coins. Aboard the small vessel he retained for his own use, he stored several hundred thousand dollars—perhaps as much as a million—so that he would not have to disturb either of his treasure caches.

For the next year or two Bowlegs appears to have led a quiet life for he was not reported at sea during that time. He couldn't resist, however, the temptation to bag some additional prizes. He rounded up another crew, and in a few short weeks the hold of his ship was bulging with chests of jewels and gold and silver coins and bars.

After several weeks at sea, during which time his ship had been in several furious fights, he headed for his lair on the Florida west coast for repairs. During a heavy gale the pirate vessel was sighted by a British warship which quickly gave chase. Billy knew that his poorly conditioned ship would never be able to outrun the British, but he had a plan in mind.

A few miles ahead there was a small harbor with a sand bar across its entrance. Billy's shallow craft could cross the bar; the warship could not. Scraping bottom several times, the pirate maneuvered his craft to the safety of the lagoon and laughed at the man of war riding the heavy waves outside the bar.

But the pirate chasers had no intention of letting Billy outwit them so easily. Small boats filled with armed marines were lowered and pulled toward the anchored pirate vessel. In order to prevent his treasure from falling into British hands, Billy decided upon a drastic, but very effective move. Gathering some equipment and supplies and a few bags of coins, he scuttled the ship in four fathoms of water. Then the pirates took to the longboat and pulled for the shore and the protective woods.

The British commander finally gave up in disgust and sailed away, and Billy and his twenty-seven marooned pirates emerged from the woods to plan their next move. It was possible to salvage a few things from the wrecked vessel, but the treasure was at the bottom and there it would stay until proper diving equipment was secured.

Billy put the pirates to work building a few shacks along the beach. The treasure was as safe at the bottom of the lagoon as it would be any place. He would simply establish a permanent camp here and salvage it at his convenience. Leaving the camp in charge of his trusted lieutenant, Pedro Bogue, Billy and two companions left for Louisiana to secure diving equipment and to bring back his family.

Several months later when Bowlegs returned with his Choctaw wife and children, only four of the twenty-five pirates still remained at the camp. Some had died of fever, others had been killed by the Indians, and the remainder had simply wandered away. Billy was short-handed and all efforts to salvage the treasure ended in failure. When his wife died of fever, Billy gave up all attempts to recover the treasure from the sunken vessel. He moved across the bay and built a log cabin. Here he lived within sight of his treasure the remainder of his life.

By the time Billy Bowlegs' children were grown he was the only member of the original pirate crew still living. His boys could see no reason for living in the woods like Indians and tried to get their father to spend some of the hidden hoard. The very thought of dipping into the treasure sent Billy into a rage. Finally the boys tried to force him to reveal where the treasure was hidden, but the aging pirate cursed them and drove them away. It was the last he ever saw of them.

During the last twelve years of his life an old friend lived in the cabin with Billy and one day the pirate actually showed the man where the treasure was buried. Upon his death, the friend was to have all the treasure, but when the friend finally got around to leading an expedition to the spot it was several years later and nature had made many changes. The landmarks and old Billy's markers were found without too much difficulty but thousands of tons of sand had drifted over the site and the treasure was never located.

Billy Bowlegs was ninety-three when he died in 1888—the last of the old Gulf pirates. During all those years he had never touched as much as one piece of eight although he would frequently visit the treasure sites and keep the markers in place. His vast treasure still rests under the shifting Florida sands, and his schooner with almost a million dollars worth of gold and silver bars in its hold still lies at the bottom of the lagoon where Billy scuttled her, covered with tons of silt and mud.

14.

LOST MINES

In every section of the United States where there has been any mining activity—and even in some areas where there have never been any mines—there are stories of lost mines and hidden caches of gold. "How could a mine get lost?" you might ask, and it is a good question.

Most of the so-called lost mines were never mines at all, in the sense that there was never any mining done. If an old prospector found a ledge of silver or a vein of gold-bearing ore and, for one reason or another, was never able to find his way back to the scene of his discovery, that became a "lost mine." In years of retelling the tale, the mine usually acquired a colorful name identifying it with some incident relative to its discovery or location such as The Lost Mine of the Little Brown Men, The Lost French Bull Ring Mine, The Lost Padre Mine, or The Lost Dutch Oven Mine. Here is a good example.

In the winter of 1849 a train of emigrants was headed for the gold fields of California. One thing was uppermost in their minds—to get there over the shortest possible route. At Salt Lake City the party heard of a shorter route to the Southwest and foolishly determined to take it. To make matters worse the map they had picked up along the way was faulty and gave no indication of the dreadful country ahead.

After many weeks of bitter hardships and constant quarreling and bickering among their members, they crossed Utah and Nevada and climbed a range of barren mountains and looked down into a desolate, salt-encrusted valley surrounded on all sides by towering mountains. The mountains about them were as yet unnamed, but later maps would appropriately label them the Funerals. The valley below them was unknown, but their own experience was soon to supply it with a fitting name—Death Valley.

Thirst and starvation sapped the strength of the hardiest pioneer. Wagons were abandoned along with their contents. The oxen were eaten and when the last of these was gone the famished emigrants turned to chewing harness straps or leather shoes. Only the stronger of the men could search the canyons of the enclosing mountains for a possible rabbit or a deer.

While camping in the foothills of the Funerals one night, one of the men in a party searching for game noted that the sight on the muzzle of his rifle was broken. He looked around for some means with which to replace it, and a whitish metallic substance in the rock near by caught his eye. Selecting a piece of the metal, he whittled and shaped a crude substitute for the missing gunsight.

No thought was given the mineral. No note was made of the location. Water and food were the only things that mattered. Those still living pushed ahead across the valley floor. The dead lay strewed behind them. Eventually a few of their number reached the little pueblo of Los Angeles. Among them was the man carrying the gun with a broken sight.

When he recovered from his terrible experience in Death Valley, this man prepared to head north to the gold fields. But his gun needed repairing. He took it to an artisan who immediately recognized the substitute sight as pure silver. "Where did this stuff come from?" asked the gunsmith. The emigrant could barely remember the details, but he did recall that a whole mountain of the metal existed!

The mine became known as the Lost Gunsight and, although the emigrant made several trips to locate the rich ore, he was never able to retrace his steps. Hundreds of men have searched—and still search—the breadth and length of Death Valley for the Lost Gunsight Mine. Some have never returned, others have come out sered to the bone from the blistering heat. None have ever found it.

Equally well known, and in the same locality, is the Lost Breyfogle Mine, which takes its name from an old prospector named Jacob Breyfogle. One day in 1864 he was found bleeding and half crazy, his bald head so badly burned it looked as if he had been scalped. He was shoeless and his clothes hung in shreds. He could make nobody understand what had happened to him for his words were gibberish.

In spite of his condition, however, Breyfogle clung desperately to a few samples of fabulously rich gold ore which he had picked up someplace during his wanderings in Death Valley. Finally he was well enough to piece together his story. One night while camping in the foothills of the valley he had been attacked by Indians. They robbed him, beat him, and left him for dead. One of his shoes was missing. He used the other for carrying water, when water could be found. Working his way slowly and painfully northward, he had come upon a hill literally covered with gold-bearing ore. He took a few samples and tried to mark the location in his mind, but he had little idea of where he had really been.

A blaze of excitement followed his tale and, led by Breyfogle, men flocked to Death Valley to locate his lost gold mine, but the parched valley still claims its secret. So many men have sought the Lost Breyfogle Mine that the term "breyfogling" became the common description of one engaged in searching for lost mines.

Many years before Arizona and New Mexico became a part of the United States, the Spanish and Indians mined the area. When the Spanish left the country they concealed their mines, hoping someday to return. With their Spanish masters gone, the Indians had little use for the gold and silver which the white man so cherished, but they, too, destroyed all evidence of the mines in the hope that the white man would lose interest in the country and stay away.

One of the most famous of the lost Spanish mines is the Lost Dutchman, somewhere in the Superstition Mountains about thirty-five miles east of Phoenix, Arizona. The story of the Lost Dutchman is a maze of conflicting facts and legend, yet it is basically authentic.

Spaniards by the name of Peralta—a rather common name in southwestern United States and northern Mexico—discovered and worked rich gold deposits in the Superstitions when the area was still a part of Old Mexico. For some reason the Peraltas decided to leave the area, perhaps because of the increasing hostility of

the Indians or because the United States was about to acquire the country through the Gadsden Purchase. At any rate the Peraltas decided to carry out as much ore as possible in one last expedition and abandon the mines.

After they had taken out all the ore that they could carry back to Mexico, the entrance to the mine, or mines, was carefully concealed, and the long train of some four hundred men and many ore-laden mules started down the mountain. Hardly were they out of sight of the mine when the Apaches swooped down from ambush in a fierce attack. There was no time to organize a defense, and the ground was soon littered with dead and dying men. Not until every Spaniard was killed did the Apaches ease the slaughter, but two young Peralta boys managed to scramble into the bushes and escape detection.

Wild-eyed with fear and trembling lest their presence be discovered, the two lads watched the Indians rifle the effects of the dead men. Then they gathered up the scattered ore and carefully hid it under piles of brush and rocks. Their work done, the Indians vanished as suddenly as they had appeared, but the two boys waited until night to start the long walk across the desert to their home in Mexico.

When the two Peralta boys had grown into young men, they took a third partner and returned to the Superstitions, aware that only they knew the secret of the family mine. They located the old tunnels without too much difficulty, but they had hardly begun to dig when the Dutchman came along.

This Dutchman was a prospector with a long white beard, and his name was Jacob Walz. He had been prospecting in the area and, fleeing a party of Indians, he stumbled upon the three Spaniards by accident. The old Dutchman knew at once that the strangers had found something and he determined to learn their secret. They became friends, and before long the Peraltas took him into their confidence and told of the mine they had reopened.

Jacob Walz waited his chance patiently. It came one evening around the campfire. The three men sat with their backs to the prospector. He quietly reached for his rifle. Three shots crashed through the canyon, and Jacob Walz was the sole possessor of the rich Peralta mine.

Walz worked the mine from 1870 to the time of his death in 1884, never bothering to file a claim. He sneaked in and out of Phoenix, where he was known by many people, living the life of a recluse and guarding his secret well. Many attempts were made to follow the old Dutchman but somehow he always managed to vanish mysteriously into thin air. Sometimes a man foolhardy enough to trail the old prospector didn't return, and Walz once admitted the killing of eight men to protect his mine.

When death was near, Walz finally told a woman who had befriended him how to reach the mine in the Superstitions. She tried many times and failed, like hundreds after her. Some men have spent most of their lives searching for the Lost Dutchman, but the Superstitions have not yet yielded their secret.

Many of the lost mines of the West were originally found by soldiers, trappers, and scouts, who picked up gold pebbles in the creek beds without making any attempt to trace the gold to its source in the hills from which it had been washed. Later, after realizing the value of their find, they failed to find their way back to the site and another "lost mine" was born.

Very few of the men who made these discoveries knew how to identify minerals and, consequently, carried around samples of rich ore without having any idea of its value. Around a campfire some night the samples would be shown to an old prospector who would recognize their value at once. Where was the sample found? Well, it was almost always impossible for the finder to return! The "mine" was lost, but the story would live to be retold over and over, each time embellished in detail.

Many an old prospector would not trust the mining laws of the time and neglected to file claims which, of course, would reveal the location of his mine. He secretly removed ore as he needed it and, when he felt the urge to move on in search of a richer mine, he concealed his find and walked away. He would talk boastfully of his mine to companions, but never reveal its location. When accident or death caught up with him, his mine became another "lost mine."

Expedition after expedition has failed to find the Lost Nigger Ben mine or the Lost San Saba, both in Texas; the Lost Adams, the Lost Frenchman, the Lost Dutchman, in Arizona; the Lost Blue Bucket in Oregon or Nevada; or the Lost Crow, the Lost Cement, and Pegleg Smith's fabulous lost mine in California. There are dozens of others—some well documented, others steeped in legend—scattered all over the West, attracting a fresh army of searchers each year.

15.

THE LOST BLUE BUCKET MINE

IN THE FALL OF 1845, four full years before James W. Marshall's discovery of gold at Sutter's Mill was to send a hundred thousand men stampeding to California, a large emigrant train of more than a hundred wagons was slowly winding its way across the deserts and canyons of northwestern Nevada, headed for the Malheur country of Oregon. These men were not miners; they hardly knew what gold was. They were farmers and laborers.

Near the present town of Beowawe, Nevada, the train split into two sections, one heading west for California, the other striking north across the Black Rock country to Oregon. Our story concerns the Oregon-bound party.

After leaving the Humboldt, the fifty wagons or so headed into a great unknown land of alkali sinks, grotesque rocks, brilliant sunsets, and mysterious mirages—a land still known by few men. Three or four days after leaving the bald,

black peak known as Black Rock, the party entered the breath-taking ranges and valleys of the Black Rock Mountains. Time after time the wagons had to be taken apart and carried up steep cliffs and then reassembled. At other places they would have to be lowered down precipices by ropes. Finally they came to a deep and rough canyon, where in places the wagons could barely scrape between the two rock walls. Down the center flowed a small inviting stream.

When the party found a suitable place along the cool waters, everyone was more than ready for a rest. Someone noted that the iron wagon tires left ruts in the shiny stuff at the bottom of the shallow stream. Knowing nothing of minerals, the men pronounced it brass and let it go at that.

The children in the party found that the shiny chunks of "brass" were nicely rounded and smooth. They made interesting playthings. While the men busied themselves with making repairs and the women prepared the meal, the youngsters romped and played in the water and picked up little piles of the yellow pebbles.

As was frequently the custom among emigrant trains, all the wagons of one party would be painted the same color as well as all the tools and equipment. Along the side of each wagon hung a pail, handy for carrying water. Many of the wagons in this train, as well as the buckets, were painted blue. One of the children secured one of the blue buckets and started filling it with the shiny rocks and pebbles. Soon the other children were following suit, and several buckets of the shiny stuff were collected. When the train stopped again, they would have something to play with.

While camped along the stream, one of the women who had been ill for several days suddenly became worse and died. She was buried near by, and a mound of rocks was piled above the grave to mark the place. At the head of the grave a pole was stuck into the ground and one of the blue buckets, still filled with the shiny yellow pebbles, was hung from it—one of thousands of similar graves soon to dot the prairies and mountains from Kansas to California.

When the train was ready to move on, the wagon master ordered the children to empty the buckets of the worthless stones. The going was bad enough, he growled, without making the oxen haul buckets of rocks across the mountains. The children reluctantly obeyed, but a few managed to smuggle some of their precious stones into the wagons. The train moved on, unaware that many of these very men would lose their lives attempting to find the spot they were leaving.

Many weeks later, while crossing the Deschutes River, the emigrants in the blue wagons came to more grief. The wagons capsized in the swollen stream, and much of their contents was washed away, including most of the stones still cherished and preserved by the children. A few, however, managed to save the shiny pebbles and these found their way into their new homes in Oregon.

Some four years later a few of the men in the party had left their Oregon homes and were at Sutter's Mill in California when gold was discovered there in 1849. They saw the shiny nuggets picked up in the millrace and knew at once that these were the same as the "brass" pebbles picked up by the children in the canyon north of Black Rock! Gold! Well, if this was gold, they knew where there was a canyon floor literally covered with it!

The men went back to Oregon to recruit some of the other settlers for the trip in search of the Black Rock gold. While there they were able to recover a few of the "blue bucket" nuggets still lying about the cabins of the settlers. There was no doubt about it—the stuff they had thought was brass was really gold!

A party of ninety men was organized for the return trip to the Black Rock country. Find the gold? Of course, they could. Any number of them remembered very well the canyon that had given them so much trouble. Who would ever forget it?

Somewhere near the Oregon-Nevada line the party of gold hunters was attacked by a band of Indians, and about half of them were killed. Of the survivors, only two men had been in the original party with the blue wagons and they alone, of course, knew the canyon's exact location. These two men became separated from the remainder of the survivors and eventually turned up in Yreka, California, in bad physical condition from the hardships they had suffered.

Both men were treated in Yreka by a doctor named Dane, but one man soon died. The other lived several weeks and, knowing that he was going to die, told Doctor Dane of the approximate location of the gold canyon and gave him directions how to get there. The doctor listened but figured that the dying man was suffering from delusions of some sort. Besides, men were always turning up with a story of losing a fabulously rich mine.

A few years later Doctor Dane, too, succumbed to gold fever and in his spare hours did a little placer-mining around Yreka. One day a trapper from the Hudson's Bay country stopped at Dane's office for treatment of a minor ailment.

When the doctor showed him a few small nuggets he had picked up around Yreka, it was the first gold the old trapper had ever seen. "If that stuff's gold," he said, "I know where there's a wagon load of it!"

The trapper told how he had wintered his horses in a canyon in the Black Rock country. When the snow had gone out in the spring, he had noted shiny pebbles in the stream. The whole stream bed was full of it! Sure, he knew how to get back there! Hadn't he spent the winter there? His detailed description of the canyon fitted perfectly the canyon described by the dying man.

The trapper agreed to accompany the doctor and a companion to the Black Rock country. Back-tracking on the dead ashes of his campfires, the three men finally climbed a peak and the old trapper pointed to two mountains rising on the horizon to the northeast. "There," said the trapper, "is the canyon of gold. It is at the base of the peak to the right, and on the west side. That is where I grazed my horses. The stream runs full in the spring, but is low in the fall."

The three men found the canyon just as the trapper and the dying man had described. From one end of the canyon to the other, in some

places only wide enough for the passage of a wagon, they searched along the stream bed. On all sides there was evidence of a recent cloudburst. Boulders and brush, freshly torn from their resting place, were piled high, and the canyon walls showed the marks of high water. There was no gold!

With their food supply running low, the three searchers finally concluded that the cloudburst and roaring waters of the flood had completely washed away all remains of the gold, or that it had been covered up by landslides. Reluctantly they gave up the search, the trapper returning to the woods, and the doctor to his practice in Yreka.

About twenty years later a boy named George Johnson and a man known as Bill Adams stopped overnight at the Malheur Indian Reservation in eastern Oregon. They fell into conversation with the friendly Indians and the subject of the lost canyon of gold came up. One of the Indians told the white men that he had once entered a canyon many miles to the south where he had found many wagon tracks and the logs used to lower the wagons over the cliffs. Proceeding down the canyon he had come across a grave marked by a pile of stones along a stream. Beside the grave was a rusted bucket. He wasn't interested in gold and hadn't looked for any, but he was certain that he was in the canyon of gold that all the white men talked about.

Did Doctor Dane's party reach the wrong canyon, after all? The Indian's description fitted the canyon with the gold nuggets, but did he fabricate the story for the benefit of the white men? It was a favorite Indian trick! At any rate, the Lost Blue Bucket Mine has never been found. The facts are more authentic than in the case of many lost mines, but hundreds of searchers have failed to locate the lonely grave beside the stream with the gold nuggets.

16.

SEMINOLE BILL'S LOST MINE

DOWN IN THE HEART OF TEXAS where the Rio Grande makes a great U-shaped dip into old Mexico the country is known as the Big Bend. It is a land of gravel-covered slopes, arroyos and washes, spectacular canyons and rugged highlands, a land of romance and legend.

The Reagan brothers—Frank, Jim, John, and Lee—came to the Big Bend country in 1884 and started ranching along the Rio Grande. Their camp was set up at the head of a canyon dipping down into the Rio Grande. It is still known as Reagan Canyon. A half-day's ride by horse from the head of this canyon is rich gold ore, lying exposed on the surface, yet none of the hundreds of men who have combed the area have been able to locate it. At least Seminole Bill said there was gold there and he had specimens to show!

The Reagan boys did their trading in Dryden or Sanderson, either one located about twenty miles from their camp headquarters on the border. One day in 1887 when Lee Reagan was in Dryden to purchase the monthly supply of bacon and beans, he was approached by a large Seminole-Negro in search of a job. He spoke very broken English and his Spanish was little better. His name, he said, was Bill Kelly, but he also answered to Seminole Bill or Santa Rosa. Why Santa Rosa? Well, he came from the country around the Santa Rosa Mountains south of Del Rio. He could ride and rope, wrangle and cook; he was a general hand.

Reagan looked the man over and hired him, no questions asked, and the two rode back to the ranch together. Seminole Bill was assigned the job of range-riding, mostly rounding up stray cows and calves. Most of the time he rode alone and frequently would be gone for several days. He was a quiet fellow and performed his job in a satisfactory manner, getting along well enough with the men in the Reagan outfit. When Bill spoke no one paid much attention to him, however, because his peculiar jargon of half-English, half-Spanish was difficult to understand.

Sitting around the campfire one night, Seminole Bill calmly announced that he had found a gold mine. "A what?" someone asked. "*Mina del oro,*" replied Bill. "*Muy oro!*" Whatever else Bill had to say was drowned by the laughter of the cowboys. The Seminole dropped the subject and crawled into his shell of silence.

A few days later Lee Reagan and Seminole Bill rode away from the camp alone in search of some stray horses. The cowhand was usually more talkative with Lee than with anyone else—perhaps it was that Lee listened better than the other boys. As they jogged along Seminole Bill told Lee that he had found gold ore a few days previously. Reagan let the man talk and then said, "Why didn't you bring in a sample of the ore?" The big cowboy shook his head and muttered something about it being bad luck to take gold like that. "You die 'fo you get home!" Reagan knew the common superstition among the Mexicans and Indians. "Forget it," he said.

Later that same morning the two riders separated and did not meet again until late evening. They were about halfway back to the camp when Lee pulled up to adjust his saddle. The Seminole raised in his saddle and peered in the distance. "That oro right over there," he said.

" 'Bout half mile!" He suggested that they ride over and take a look. Reagan pulled his watch from his pocket. "No time for gold," he said. "We better be making tracks for camp." Seminole Bill mumbled something about getting the gold for himself, and they rode on.

Some time later the entire Reagan outfit was in Dryden loading a bunch of cattle for the eastern markets. Seminole Bill had acted unusually quiet for several days, but Reagan thought a few drinks would fix him up. When the freight pulled out Seminole Bill was aboard, and the Reagans were short one cowhand.

Seminole Bill stayed with the train all the way to San Antonio. His first act was to look up Locke Campbell, an employee of the Southern Pacific Railroad. Somewhere Bill had met Campbell and trusted him. The railroader was away on a run, but Bill waited for his return. Whatever he had on his mind, it was mighty important business.

Campbell could see at once that the big cowboy was nervous, and he appeared to be relieved when he handed over the sample of ore he carried. "Why, this stuff is rich, Seminole," Campbell said. "Where did it come from?" Seminole Bill told how he had found the ore on the Reagan ranch. He wanted the railroader to have it assayed.

Puzzled over the cowboy's sudden disappearance, the Reagans were even more amazed when Seminole Bill rode into camp one day and asked for his job back. He was put to work, and everyone noted that some change had come over him. What was eating Seminole Bill? No one knew and he wasn't talking.

Seminole Bill was at the camp about a week when he took one of the horses and said that he was going to ride into Sanderson. The station agent at Sanderson was the last man on record to see Seminole Bill alive. The cowboy left his horse with the agent, asked him to turn it over to the Reagans, and dropped out of sight.

Shortly after Seminole Bill's second mysterious disappearance, one of the Reagan boys rode into Sanderson to pick up the mail. He was handed a letter addressed to Bill Kelly in care of the Reagan ranch. It bore a San Antonio postmark and Reagan, thinking it might be important, opened it. The letter was signed by Locke Campbell and contained an assay report. The ore Bill had left with him was rich in gold!

Lee Reagan was certain that he could ride right to the spot where Seminole Bill had said the mine was but a half mile away. That was when Reagan first regretted the fact that he had not listened to the cowboy. He combed the area but he could find nothing. The next best thing was to find the missing cowboy, and he started by having a talk with Locke Campbell. But Campbell knew nothing of the big Seminole's whereabouts, nor had Bill given him any idea of the mine's location. All they knew was that the Indian had found gold on the Reagan ranch.

Locke Campbell spent a good many years searching for the missing cowboy. Several hundred miles away on an Indian reservation he located the missing man's aging mother. She related that Seminole Bill had come home a few weeks before and that he had samples of rich ore with him. He had then left and had not been heard from. Campbell offered a reward for information about the big Indian cowboy, but this produced no results. He hired a prospector to search the Reagan ranch area. This, too, failed.

From time to time reports came in that Seminole Bill was seen in this place and that, but while Campbell spent a small fortune in running down the clues, the real Bill Kelly never showed up.

There are those who contend that Seminole Bill never found a gold mine, but had picked up some pieces of ore dropped by fleeing bandits. Others insist that fleeing bandits don't carry heavy ore with them. Some believed that Seminole had deliberately played a trick on the Reagans. Why he would do so is hardly clear. As far as is known he had no grudge against the ranchers. On the other hand, there are men who think that Bill found the ore along a ledge which later caved in or was covered by a cloudburst, hiding the ore from view. Why did he not return to claim his treasure? Perhaps he was afraid that the Reagans would beat him out of it. Perhaps he really believed that old Spanish superstition that gold belongs only to the man who put it there and "you die 'fo you get home" if you touch it. Again, Seminole Bill may have talked to too many people about his secret and was killed by someone trying to force the location from him.

Whatever the cause of the mysterious disappearance of Bill Kelly, the Lost Seminole Bill Mine still intrigues men and the search for it still goes on. Lee Reagan often said later that he could kick himself from here to kingdom come for having been more concerned with the time of day than a gold mine! Let this be a lesson to all skeptics. When someone says there is gold in them hills—take a look!

17.

THE LOST CABIN MINE

THE MOST FAMOUS lost mine story of the Rockies is that of the twice-lost gold mine somewhere on Crazy Woman Creek in the Big Horn Mountains of Wyoming. There are several versions of the story, but they agree except for minor details, and all involve Indians.

Allen Hulbert was a quiet, sensible citizen of Wisconsin until, like a lot of other men of the time, he was stricken with gold fever and left for California. He found no gold and finally ended up in Walla Walla, Washington, where he took up with two other roving spirits named Cox and Jones. All prospectors at heart, the trio decided to explore for gold in the Yellowstone country, and in due time they plunged into the wild and rugged, Indian-filled mountains, panning and prospecting as they slowly worked their way eastward.

The three men crossed the raging Yellowstone, the canyon of the Big Horn, and into the heart of a country that few white men had ever seen. Then, in the vicinity of the upper forks of twisting Crazy Woman Creek they struck pay dirt. Slowly they followed the yellow flecks until they came to the mother lode and here they

sank a shaft seven feet to bedrock. They worked the rich find until the changing weather forced them to think about approaching winter. They whip-sawed logs and built a crude cabin, surrounded by a stockade, where they spent the long winter.

As soon as possible the next spring they were at the mine again, and every day saw their fortune in nuggets increase in size. With only the crudest of implements the three men were taking several hundred dollars a day from their mine.

One day that summer, Hulbert left his two companions at the mine and returned to the cabin for something he had forgotten. No sooner was he out of sight than the sound of two gun shots brought him to a sudden halt. Stealthily he sneaked back to the mine. The bodies of Cox and Jones were stretched out on the mine tailings and a band of Indians was going through the gruesome motions of scalping them. Panic-stricken, Hulbert immediately set out for the southeast, pausing only at the cabin long enough to bury what gold he could not carry with him.

After eighteen days of dangerous travel on foot Hulbert reached one of the great transcontinental routes to the gold fields at the point where Casper is now located. Here he met a wagon train of gold seekers and, undismayed, he joined them. Other than his two dead partners, they were the first white men he had seen in almost two years.

Hulbert could see no point in seeking gold in California when he already knew where there was a rich strike much nearer. He was almost mobbed when he offered to lead the party to his mine, and he was close to being torn limb from limb when, after weeks of fruitless search, he finally had to admit that he was lost. The angry party scattered, and Allen Hulbert was last heard of in Virginia City, Montana, sometime around 1864.

In spite of the wildness of the country and the hostility of the Indians, white men continued to penetrate into the Big Horn country, and it was inevitable that someone would stumble upon the crude cabin and the body of ore so large and rich that it was hardly believable.

Three unnamed prospectors found the lost cabin and worked it one summer until their tools gave out. They buried what gold they could not take with them and headed east for the winter, intending to return in the spring.

Floating down the Little Big Horn on a raft at night, the bark of a curious dog betrayed their presence to a band of Indians. The three men were captured, and two were almost immediately killed. The third managed somehow to escape.

One day in the fall of 1865 a lone man, bleeding and half starved, stumbled into the stockade of old Fort Reno on Powder River. He showed some pieces of gold to the commander of the post and told of his escape from the Indians. The officers refused to believe his story and placed him under arrest. Later released, he spent the winter at Fort Laramie and organized a party of ten men, all of whom left the next spring to locate the lost mine. Not one of them was ever heard from again, and although countless expeditions have searched for the cabin in the Big Horns, no trace of it has ever been found.

With these bare facts alone there might be little basis for the persistent belief that gold exists in the Big Horn Mountains of Wyoming in the fabulous quantities described by the two men who actually worked it. However, the written testimony of two other men, whose in-

tegrity must be acknowledged, indicates that the Big Horns do hold a secret that someone may someday discover.

Father Jeanne Pierre de Smet, the Jesuit missionary who roamed in and out of the Rockies for some twenty years, knew gold when he saw it and he knew the Rocky Mountain country well. When he was told of the sensational gold finds in California he shrugged off the news saying he knew where there was gold in astounding quantities this side of the Rockies.

When pressed for further information, the Jesuit related that friendly Indians had showed him gold deposits. He had warned the red men

the rugged mountains of Wyoming.

James Bridger, guide, mountaineer, and trader, was leading the Reynolds Expedition across northern Wyoming in the summer of 1859. One day he stopped at a small stream in the Big Horn Mountains for a drink, and he was amazed to find handfuls of gold nuggets in the pure, cold water. He scooped up a number of the nuggets and showed them to Captain Reynolds. Both agreed that it was gold, but Reynolds feared that the news would stampede his soldiers and ruin his army career. He ordered Bridger to throw the stuff away and keep the news to himself.

that their country would be devastated if the white men ever learned their secret. The Indians, already knowing something of the white man's way, agreed, and de Smet swore that he would never reveal where the gold was. When he died in 1872 he took his secret with him. It is believed that Father de Smet had seen gold in

Bridger obeyed and, although he later told the story to numerous people, he apparently made no attempt to locate the gold a second time. He often said that he cared nothing for wealth and, when he died in 1881, the mystery of the Lost Cabin Mine was as deep and as baffling as ever.

18.

THE LOST LAKE OF GOLD

ONE NIGHT in the late autumn of 1849 a group of miners were wetting their whistles in Bill McGhee's saloon at Downie's Flat on the north fork of the Yuba River in northern California. McGhee's place, sheltered from the weather in a tent, was noted locally for a drink called "cornmeal fixin's," an unbelievable concoction of brandy, water, and cornmeal, but the boys liked it.

The night was stormy, and every time the door opened a blast of winter wind blew in. It was no time to be on the trail, yet suddenly in stumbled a man who had evidently traveled a long distance. His shredded clothing was crusted with ice and his face was gaunt with hunger. He limped to the bar and ordered food and liquor.

When the stranger was filled with food and warmed with several brandies, he talked, and what he had to say stirred the crowded saloon with excitement. He started by sketchily filling in his background. His name was Stoddard—Richard Stoddard—and he was from Philadelphia, where he had been a schoolmaster and newspaper editor. He had come west in the gold rush, and he and a companion had joined up with a wagon train, crossing the prairies without incident.

Along the Humboldt in Nevada someone had told the wagon master of a new and easier pass —the Jim Beckwourth Pass—across the mountains. His outfit took the new trail and nothing but hard luck followed. Near Big Meadows (now Lake Almanor) the train ran out of meat. Deer were plentiful in the region, and Stoddard and his companion left the camp to replenish the meat supply.

They had hunted without any success for several hours and decided to return to camp. It was then that they realized they were lost! They walked aimlessly until nightfall, unable to recognize a single landmark. In the morning

73

it was the same. The vast wilderness had swallowed them up. For days they wandered in circles, hoping to pick up a trail, praying for the sound of a human voice.

Their position was desperate. Winter was coming on. Their food was gone. Their last ammunition had been spent. At last they came to the headwaters of a small stream and had the presence of mind to follow its downward course. Along its banks they found berries and roots which kept them alive. Eventually it brought them to a small lake, ten to fifteen acres in area, Stoddard thought, and surrounded by mountains. Here they camped for the night.

While kneeling for a drink of water at the lake's edge the next morning the two men noticed yellow pebbles scattered about underneath the water. They scooped up some of the stones and knew at once that they were gold nuggets! The floor of the lake was literally covered with gold!

With pockets and knapsacks filled, the two men noted carefully the location of the lake and its surrounding landmarks, resolving that they would remember

the air. Indians! In the first onrush of the red men, Stoddard's companion was killed, but Stoddard managed to crawl into a crevice made by several large boulders and so escape detection. It was here that he first noticed the arrow wound in his leg, painful but not serious.

The days that followed were horrible nightmares. The wounded leg became infected. His strength was spent and, unable to carry the knapsack of nuggets any longer, he scooped out a hole beneath a rock and cached it. Later he was forced to empty his pockets of all but a few specimens. Now, just as all hope seemed fruitless, he had stumbled into the mining camp.

The cold eyes that stared at him told of the

the area well enough to be able to return. They continued their way down-stream, jubilant over their discovery, but still desperately in need of food.

On the following day the weather appeared to be clearing and they found some edible roots which subdued their gnawing hunger. They were picking their way through an area littered with boulders when an arrow whistled through

skepticism with which his story was received. Stoddard reached into his pocket and brought out several gold nuggets. "Here is proof!" he said, throwing them on the table for all to see. They were smooth and round with no traces of adhering river gravel or mother earth, and anyone could see that they were worth from $8 to $25 each.

He exposed the swollen wound on his leg.

"Here is more proof!" he said. "Now who can call me a liar?" None could. The miners who had thought him raving mad now pressed him for more details. Where had he been? He had no idea, of course. How far had he traveled? Perhaps fifty or seventy miles; he wasn't sure. Could he retrace his steps? That he could, he was certain, and he would as soon as he was able to travel.

News of the lake of gold swept the mining camps like the blizzards from the north, and the pebbles grew in size with each repeating until they were as large as goose eggs. The Marys-

ville *Transcript* embellished the story with rare imagination, reporting that the Indians of the gold lake region used blocks of pure gold for council seats and made their arrowheads and fish hooks from the same common stuff. Even with snow falling in the mountain passes men waited anxiously for Richard Stoddard to recover and lead them to the lake with the gold bottom. When Stoddard was well, however, there was thirty feet of snow in the Sierras. He departed for San Francisco to spend the winter, promising that he would return in the spring.

True to his word, the Philadelphian appeared at Nevada City early in the spring of 1850 and attempted secretly to secure financial backing from twenty-five men. To secure the backing was easy. Hundreds of men would have backed him with money. To do it secretly, however, was an impossibility. The whole country buzzed with excitement and preparation. The lake of gold was the new El Dorado!

When Stoddard and his twenty-five backers took the trail quietly and unexpectedly in the middle of the night, they were alone. In the morning they saw five hundred men behind them, beating a trail a bulldozer could have followed. Miners who were taking out a pound of gold dust a day dropped their claims and joined in the search. They traveled on foot and by mule, carrying their food and tools, floun-

dering through the icy slush by day, freezing in the biting winds at night.

After three weeks of travel up the Yuba's north fork, down into the Mohawk, Red Clover, Round, Sierra, Genesee and Humbug valleys and all the lands between, the cavalcade reached an isolated valley near the summit of the Sierra. For three days they remained there, Stoddard desperately seeking a familiar skyline, a peak, or a boulder that would set him on the right track. There were nasty rumblings from the miners. Could their suspicions be true?

Finally Stoddard admitted his bewilderment. He was completely lost and confused. The revolution was about to break. That night the miners held council and charged the Philadelphian with deliberately misguiding them in order to protect the find for himself. In the morning they issued their ultimatum: find Gold Lake in twenty-four hours or else!

Stoddard was a well-educated man and a fluent talker. "God willing," he declared, he would find the gold or die in the attempt. The mob wanted gold and, God willing or not, they would have it or his life. With or without divine approval, Stoddard concluded that twenty-four hours was a pitifully short time to locate a ten-acre lake in the tumbled wilderness of the Sierra Nevadas. He slipped out of camp that night and somehow made his way past the guard that had been posted and without disturbing the restless mules. If he succeeded in making his way out of the mountains, he never again appeared in the northern mining camps. The valley from which he fled the angry miners is known to this day as Last Chance Valley, and somewhere in that vicinity—if Richard Stoddard told the truth—is the Lost Lake of Gold.

But Gold Lake had its aftermath. The fabulous strikes at Rich Bar, Nelson Point, and other places were made by men seeking Stoddard's lake, and the actual settlement of Sierra, Plumas and Yuba counties was a result of the gold lake excitement.

One day in the fall of 1853 a well-known character in the Feather River region, Francis Lingard, appeared in John B. Carrington's store on Hopkins Creek and purchased supplies which he paid for with a nugget worth $100. Later he made other purchases, paying for them with nuggets of similar size. This went on for several weeks. Soon the miner was broke and, seeking a grubstake, he took Carrington into his confidence.

He told the storekeeper that he had been prospecting in the High Sierras during the pre-vious year. There was little water in the hills because of a prolonged drought, and one afternoon he was overjoyed to see a small lake some distance ahead of him. He rushed forward to quench his thirst and, falling to his knees, he discovered the bottom of the lake to be covered with gold nuggets.

He slept that night close to the lake and in the morning, after gathering all the gold he could carry, he resumed his trip to Nelson Point for supplies. He had not gone far when he found that he had more gold than he could carry over the rough country ahead of him. Most of the nuggets were cached at the base of a tall pine.

While he was at Nelson Point, the drought broke and for ten days there was a steady downpour of rain. As soon as possible he took the trail again but was unable to locate either his cache of nuggets or the lake of gold. The long rain had obliterated his trail and had changed the appearance of the country with landslides and floods. He hunted without success until his supply of nuggets gave out. Now he was broke.

Carrington grubstaked the prospector who continued the search until winter drove him from the mountains. Experienced men searched the region carefully in the years that followed and all finally agreed that the heavy rains had

probably filled the lake to a new level and hid the gold nuggets from view. Whether this was Stoddard's lake or not is anybody's guess.

While the story of Stoddard's lost lake was still stimulating news in the mining camps of northern California, along came Old Caleb Greenwood with a story all his own. He had a talent for rich and variegated profanity and a great contempt for Spaniards and Indians. At his advanced age he was as tough as the ancient buckskins he wore and despite his rheumy eyes he was a dead shot with a rifle. An ex-trapper and scout, he was engaged in packing and trading among the mining camps, living with his two half-breed boys, John and Britain, the sons of a Crow squaw.

One day Old Caleb stumbled into a camp where everyone was talking about the gold nuggets that had been found in the bed of a near-by creek. "I know where there's plenty of that stuff," said Caleb. Everyone listened. "A few years back I camped with my two boys on the shore of a mountain lake where that stuff was thicker'n hairs on a bearskin. Boys played marbles with it and built little piles of it into forts. When we left, we just kicked 'em over and let 'em lay."

Well, where was the lake? Caleb obliged as if he had been there yesterday. You go up over Bear Valley to Two Mile, then over a ridge straight east to another valley, and then over a lot of ridges and hills to the valley with the lake of gold nuggets. If anybody wanted to go there, he'd tell his son John how to guide them to the spot. Anyone interested could put up a grubstake and leave a sum of cash in advance with Old Caleb for his trouble!

A syndicate was formed and, in addition to buying John Greenwood a handsome pack train, it gave Old Caleb a generous cash reward. One of the syndicate members was a man fresh from San Francisco. His name was Henry de Groot. Instead of accompanying the expedition, de Groot hired a Norwegian sailor to stand in for him.

Within a month the prospecting party straggled back to Greenwood's camp, ragged, destitute, and hungry. They were disgusted and angry. When they complained to Old Caleb that he had flimflammed them of their money, he merely replied: "John must have missed the right place. The stuff is sure there!"

De Groot determined to be repaid for his loss. After taking all the abuse he could stand, Caleb offered to settle the matter with a duel. De Groot walked away.

On maps of California you will find several Gold Lakes, but none of them has ever produced as much as an ounce of gold unless, of course, as many miners thought, high waters have covered Stoddard's fabulous gold nuggets from view.

19.

BURNT WAGONS AND BURIED TREASURE

UNLESS SOMEONE DELIBERATELY sets out to hide the remains of a burnt wagon, the metal parts and even the hardwood spokes and hubs will remain visible for many years. The old emigrant trails of the West are still littered with pieces of iron and wood from burnt and abandoned wagons. Each tells a story, usually one of tragedy.

But what have burnt wagons to do with buried treasure, you may ask. It is this. The great movement of people across the plains, mountains, and deserts took place in wagons, covered or uncovered, but wagons of all descriptions. It was the only mode of travel in which a man could take his family and their belongings. Most of the families moving into the great unknown West were moving for keeps. They did not expect to go back, and so they took all their possessions with them, including their wealth. When their wagon had to be abandoned for any reason, their wealth, too heavy to transport otherwise, was likely to be buried near it.

Of the many reasons why wagons were frequently burned or abandoned, the principal one was the fact that the hardships of the journey had been underestimated and the oxen simply gave out before the end of the journey. Oxen also died of disease, or they were killed off or stolen by the Indians. Sometimes it was necessary for the emigrants to kill the oxen for food. No matter what the reason, without the oxen, the wagons had to be abandoned and with them many of the family possessions.

If a family happened to be fortunate enough, the women and children would be taken into a friend's wagon, but there was never room for more than a few prized family possessions. In pioneer days practically all wealth was in gold because people did not believe in the soundness of paper money and it was difficult to dispose of. Therefore, many of the wagons making their painful way across the western territory carried a considerable amount of wealth in gold coins.

When it was necessary to cache a quantity of gold, the natural thing to do was to burn the wagon over the burial site, for this not only marked the spot for many, many years but disguised it as well.

It was also the common practice of early travelers passing through dangerous country to bury their wealth every night. Usually they dug a hole, put the treasure in it, and built the evening campfire over the spot. If they were robbed during the night by bandits or attacked by Indians, the chances of losing their gold were lessened.

In April 1846, a party of emigrants led by Jacob and George Donner and James F. Reed set out from Illinois for California. All three families were well to do and had the finest wagons obtainable. Their oxen were the best and their wagons were loaded down with trinkets, jewelry, expensive textiles for trade, books and pictures, fine furniture, and many rare items that people of their background would want but could not obtain in California. Besides the wives and children, the wagons carried several thousand dollars in gold coins.

All went fairly well until the party reached the barren salt flats of western Utah. Perfectly flat and without vegetation of any kind, this area looks like a dead sea encrusted with a hard layer of salt, and so it actually is. On the parched drive across the salt desert thirty-six head of oxen were lost through careless herding and four wagons had to be abandoned, including one of the heavy Donner vehicles.

The rumor has persisted that the party buried a considerable quantity of gold near the abandoned wagons a few miles east of Silver Island, a lonely peak rising along the western fringe of the salt desert. Parts of old wagon boxes, wheels, axles, log irons, broken bottles, skeletons of dead oxen, and other debris may still be seen along the desert trail, but repeated searches have failed to uncover the buried treasure.

Later, while crossing the High Sierras the Donner party was caught in an unusually early snowstorm and thirty-six of the eighty-one members of the party died of exhaustion and hunger before they were finally rescued. More of the Donner treasure was buried during the tragic Sierra crossing, but most of this was recovered many years later.

In 1850 a party of emigrants seeking a short cut across the mountains to the California coast, came upon a field of corn, pumpkins, and beans planted by the Paiute Indians about forty miles northwest of Las Vegas, Nevada. The emigrants were running low on food supplies and helped

themselves. When the angry Paiutes protested the raiding of their fields, the easterners drove them away.

After the emigrant train had left the spot, the Indians held council and decided to follow the white men and take their revenge. At a place now called Burnt Wagons, about seven miles northwest of Death Valley Junction in the heart of Death Valley, the Indians sneaked up on the emigrants while they were camped at night. Before they were discovered they had driven off most of the travelers' horses and oxen. In the fight that resulted one white man was killed, a jeweler from Illinois.

wagons were found by a party who knew nothing of the buried treasure. When they returned to the scene, the remains of the wagons were again obliterated.

In 1853 a wealthy party consisting of one heavy wagon and several mule riders left Yuma, Arizona, to cross the Colorado Desert to San Diego. In the wagon was a large quantity of gold coins and silver plate, which was to be the means of opening a new business on the Coast.

Instead of following the regular trail through Carrizo, the party skirted to the north in search of a shorter route. One night they made camp

The jeweler had been going west to open a new business in California and he had had with him a great quantity of gold, jewelry, and watches. Two holes were dug in the desert floor. In one was placed the body of the jeweler. In the other was buried his gold and jewelry. Over the two holes the wagons that the emigrants were now forced to abandon were burned.

Many years later a relative of the dead jeweler tried to locate the grave and treasure, but without success. Shifting sands had covered the remains of the wagons. Sometime later king bolts, iron plates, and other bits of the burned

in the lower reaches of Borego Valley and, following the usual practice, they buried their treasure and built the campfire over the spot. They then bedded down, expecting to get an early start in the morning.

Just before dawn they awoke to find themselves surrounded by Indians. They fought from behind their wagon as long as possible, but the Indians circled the camp, and they were soon forced to take cover inside. The Indians fired the wagon and, one by one, the emigrants were killed as they emerged. The treasure is still there, marked by the remains of a burnt wagon, but no one has ever located the site.

Still another burnt wagon is sought in the vicinity of Signal Hill in San Diego County, California. A party was headed east after a successful prospecting trip in the gold fields. They carried their gold dust with them, securely bound in leather pouches. They, too, buried their treasure at night, were surprised by Indians, and were all killed.

A group of Mexicans who had served with the bandit, Joaquín Murietta, were returning to Sonora with the loot from their many robberies and holdups. In the hills east of Carrizo in San Diego County, they were attacked by Indians and killed to the last man. The red men gathered up the treasure, took the small trinkets that attracted them, and placed the rest in large *ollas* which they cached under the projecting rock of a near-by ledge. Returning to the scene of the slaughter, they burned the wagons.

Not every burnt wagon, of course, marks the burial place of treasure, but experienced treasure hunters have learned to follow the trail of the burnt wagons and to poke into the earth for possible treasure. As a boy I lived along the old Oregon Trail where it followed the Platte River near the Wyoming-Nebraska line. For many miles I followed the wagon tracks, still rutted deep in the prairie sod, still marked by the occasional grave of a dead pioneer.

There was one particular spot at the western extremity of Mitchell Pass in the shadows of Scott's Bluff where pieces of old iron and wood were scattered about in great confusion. Knowing nothing of the significance of burnt wagons at the time, I did not return until many years later to investigate. The old wagon ruts were still there, but not a trace of the burnt wagons could I find. Could someone have beaten me to the treasure?

20.

STAGECOACHES AND HOLDUPS

"THROW DOWN THAT BOX!" was the highway-man's command that every stagecoach driver feared for it meant a gun battle—surrender the treasure box or fight it out!

Before the coming of the railroads to the mining camps of the West practically all of the gold and silver bullion had to be carried out by stagecoaches operated by various express companies. Except when an especially large shipment of gold was being carried, the stages also carried passengers, and a ride on one was, at best, a dangerous and exciting business.

Most of the stagecoaches of the early West were known as Concord coaches because they were built in Concord, New Hampshire, by the famous firm of Abbot, Downing & Company. They were heavy, rugged vehicles, built to take the terrific jarring and jolting of wilderness roads. It was often said that a Concord coach never broke down—it just wore out from the miles that it covered.

Probably the most embattled vehicle that ever traveled in time of peace, the Concord coach was also one of the most beautiful carriages ever built. The scarlet body was made of the finest hardwoods and was richly ornamented with gilded curlicues. Both door panels were usually painted with landscape vistas as well as the identifying name of the stage line.

With properly spaced relays of six-horse teams, the stagecoach could travel one hundred miles or more a day through dusty plains, across burning deserts and through winding mountain passes, fording streams, bouncing over boulders, braving a hail of Indian arrows, or racing a determined bandit gang. More often than not the stage got through to its destination.

Riding the front seat, exposed to bullets, arrows, and the weather, the driver held sway. He was the boss of the stage—its conductor and policeman alike. With his long whip he could pick a fly off the ear of a lead horse, and he could maneuver his vehicle around impossible mountain roads with incredible ease. He was a master and mighty proud of his profession.

Beside the driver sat a guard called a "shotgun messenger." He was hired by the express company and his duty was to see that the express got through. Picked for their courage and skill with a gun, the old stagecoach guards were all that real men of the West were supposed to be—fearless dead shots.

Across the guard's knee rested a double-barreled shotgun, a type of weapon favored for its deadly spread of buckshot. But the guard was also plenty handy with revolver or rifle.

The express box that held the treasure shipment was usually carried in the forward boot, a leather-covered compartment immediately beneath the driver's seat. Mail and other baggage was carried in the rear boot, a similar but larger compartment overhanging the rear wheels of the stage.

Although the stagecoach was equipped with dim candle-power headlights which cast hardly enough light to make a shadow, the stage usually traveled in the dark at night. The headlights made too good a target for the driver and guard. Besides, they did little good.

The stage driver carried a long tin horn on which he blew a single blast when approaching a narrow mountain curve. The driver of an approaching stage would answer with two blasts to signify that he had heard the warning signal. If two stages met on a narrow grade, the "up" stage would unhitch its teams, and two men would grab the tongue and roll the vehicle downhill to a place where the two stages could safely pass each other.

Each stage could crowd in nine passengers, and while it wasn't a comfortable ride by present-day standards, it was considered somewhat luxurious at the time. A Concord stage weighed about 2400 pounds and cost about $2400—one dollar per pound. The three stage teams were selected from the best horses available, matched as to color and size, and chosen for their endurance. A driver and his passengers' lives might depend upon his horses' ability to outrun a band of yelling Indians or bandits.

The driver's run was usually about fifty miles, from a home station to a home station, where there was usually a hotel of sorts, a telegraph station, and a blacksmith shop. Between home stations there were division stations at intervals of about ten miles. Extra horses and repair facilities were located at all home and division stations.

Treasure carried by the stages usually consisted of gold dust or gold and silver bullion. It was carried in a steel box equipped with a heavy lock. The guard received it from the express agent at the point of shipment, signed a receipt for its contents, and just before the run started, placed it aboard the stage. From that point until it was delivered at its destination or turned over to a relief guard, he was responsible for its safe conduct. He was expected to guard the treasure with his life if necessary—and he often did.

Almost every stage out of the mining camps carried treasure, and the Concords were attractive prey for the bands of highwaymen who infested the country. In a lonely spot, just over the brow of a hill or around the sharp bend of a curve, the road agents waited. When the stage appeared they shouted "Halt!" If the driver didn't pull up at once, a bullet dropped one of the lead horses. Into the road jumped the masked men, guns leveled. "Throw down that box!" was the command. If the guard complied by hauling the treasure box from the boot and throwing it to the ground, the highwaymen might order the stage on its way without further gunplay and the passengers could consider themselves very lucky. Seldom were the passengers robbed.

If the guard resisted and answered the command with a blazing blast from his shotgun, the battle was on and passengers huddled in a heap on the floor until a decision was reached. The bandits did not always win the treasure; in fact, more often than not they met their match in the fearlessness of the cool guard.

So many attempts were made to hold up the stages carrying treasure out of the richer mining camps that the horses are said to have learned to stop automatically at certain places where holdups frequently occurred!

All kinds of tricks were resorted to by the express companies to outwit the bandits. One express messenger filled his treasure chest with live rattlesnakes, deliberately permitting a band of highwaymen to capture it. Imagine the dismay of those surprised bandits when they pried off the lid and saw the mass of writhing snakes!

The silver of the rich Candaleria Mine in California was cast into 500-pound balls after repeated holdups had plagued the company. Thereafter the befuddled bandits in the area turned their attention elsewhere, but not until one of them had sent word to the express company that the action was unsportsmanlike!

When the Homestake Mining Company began shipping vast quantities of gold bullion out of the Black Hills of South Dakota to the rail head at Sidney, Nebraska, so many holdups were attempted that the stage company had a special stage built for the journey.

It differed from other stages in that its center seat was removed to make room for the steel treasure chests, and it was armor-plated with loopholes for the guards to shoot from. Although it was officially known as the Treasure Express,

the stage was nicknamed "Old Ironsides."

Old Ironsides' guard consisted of from five to eight messengers, depending upon the size of the treasure shipment. One guard rode in advance of the stage, one brought up the rear, and one rode flank on each side of the stage. All were heavily armed and instructed to "shoot to kill" at the first sign of an attack.

Before its job of carrying treasure was turned over to the railroads, Old Ironsides had hauled $60,000,000 in gold out of the Black Hills. The value of each cargo ranged from $100,000 to $200,000, although a shipment valued at $350,-000 was carried one day in 1877. On that day, thirteen men guarded the stage on its entire journey. Old Ironsides was battered and bruised but only once was its precious cargo ever lost to highwaymen. That is a story in itself.

21.

THE BURIED TREASURE OF OLD IRONSIDES

ON SEPTEMBER 28, 1878, about 400 pounds of gold bricks, each stamped with the name of the Homestake Mining Company and the code number of the shipment, were placed aboard the Treasure Express for the run from Deadwood City, South Dakota, to Sidney, Nebraska.

Supervising the loading of the treasure cargo was Scott Davis, the captain of the guards and a trusted employee with a reputation for cool courage.

On the box, impatient to get going, sat Big Gene Barnett, an old hand at stage driving and one of the best horsemen in the West. Inside the stage with the treasure was the veteran guard, Bill Smith. Across from him sat a frail lad from Missouri, Gail Hill, who had been selected for his cool daring in a previous holdup attempt.

Although it was not customary to haul passengers on the Treasure Express, a man named Hugh Campbell was permitted to ride on this trip. He sat inside with the two guards.

Ordinarily from five to nine guards would have accompanied the rich shipment, but the express company had grown careless and had not bothered to round up more than three guards.

When Scott Davis mounted the box with the driver he turned to Big Gene and said, "Let's go!" Big Gene slapped the reins and gave a loud yell, and the stage lurched ahead.

All went well the first day as the stage rattled and bumped around the northern edge of the Black Hills and across the line into eastern Wyoming. A few miles ahead was the Canyon Springs Station, a relay point where the horses

86

would be exchanged for fresh ones. It was a wild and remote location at the head of a heavily timbered canyon, and all around it the mountains grew thick with pine trees.

John Miner was the tender at the Canyon Springs Station. It was his duty to tend the horses and to have fresh teams harnessed and ready to transfer to the stage with but a few minutes' loss of time. About a half hour or so before the treasure express was due he was sitting on a bench in front of the old log stable reading a paper that a passenger had left with him.

The road was frequently traveled so Miner was not surprised when a lone horseman rode up and asked for a drink of water. "Sure," the stock tender answered, going into the small room that served as his quarters. When he returned seconds later he was looking down the barrel of the stranger's six-shooter.

"Back into the barn!" snapped the man. As Miner complied, three more men rode up, and the tender could see that they meant plenty of trouble. Securely tied to a stall partition, Miner started counting off the seconds. The stage was due in thirty minutes. An ambush awaited it!

As the stage emerged from around a curve in the thickly studded pines, Big Gene Barnett gave his usual loud whoop to attract Miner's attention. There was no answer. The stage rumbled to a stop beside the relief teams which stood in their usual place. It seemed awfully quiet to Barnett, but still nothing looked too suspicious to him.

Big Gene threw the reins to the ground and jumped down. At the same moment young Gail Hill stepped from the stage and started toward the barn. A roaring fusillade of shots came from the cracks in the logs. Hill whirled and slumped to the ground. Big Gene Barnett raced around to the far side of the horses to take cover.

Inside the coach the passenger, Hugh Campbell, was dead on the seat, a bullet through his heart. Bill Smith writhed on the floor, temporarily blinded with a flying splinter in his eye.

At the second the shooting started, Scott Davis leaped to the ground on the far side of the stage and took cover behind a near-by pine tree. He motioned frantically to Big Gene to get the stage moving. At this moment one of the bandits, seeing that the stage might get away, raced from the barn to head off the move. Davis dropped him with a shot in the stomach. A second bandit came dashing from the barn and dead-shot Davis halted him in his tracks with a slug through the head.

A third bandit succeeded in reaching Barnett and, using Big Gene as a shield, closed in on

Davis. Afraid of killing the stage driver, Davis saw that the situation was helpless and took off through the pine trees for help. Several miles down the road he met a party of four men riding up to see what had delayed the treasure coach.

The riders galloped into Canyon Springs Station with drawn guns, but it was too late. The bandits had gathered up their wounded companion and had fled. There on the ground, locks broken open, were the empty treasure chests! Old Ironsides had at last been successfully robbed!

William Ward, superintendent of the stage line and an acting deputy U. S. Marshal, took up the trail of the escaped bandits and traced them to a ranch several miles away where they had purchased a spring wagon and a team of horses. Later on, freighters along the road to Rapid City reported seeing a spring wagon carrying four men. It was headed east and one of the men appeared to be ill.

Ward persisted in the chase and finally came upon an abandoned spring wagon. He concluded that the wounded man had died and that the gold bars had probably been buried somewhere along the escape route. But Ward was determined to capture the outlaws, whom he now identified as members of the Carey gang, including Jim Carey, Al Speer, Doug Goodale, and an unidentified man. Frank McBride had been killed by Scott Davis at the scene of the robbery.

For weeks Ward stuck doggedly to the trail, but finally at the little town of Atlantic in western Iowa he lost the scent completely. He was about ready to give up and return to Deadwood City when he was strolling down the street and happened to glance in a bank window.

Resting there in the window were two gold bars. Nothing so unusual about that except that these gold bars were stamped with the name of the Homestake Mine and the code number of the shipment lost in the Canyon Springs robbery!

Ward casually introduced himself to the president of the bank and inquired about the bars in the window. The banker's name was John Goodale. Yes, he admitted, the bars were from the Homestake Mine. His son Douglas had worked there and had asked to be paid off in gold bars, thinking they would make an interesting exhibit for the bank.

Ward thanked the banker and went promptly to the local sheriff. Douglas Goodale was arrested and started back to Deadwood City by train. He confessed his part in the robbery and stated that the treasure was too heavy to carry and had been buried a few miles from the robbery. Such had been their hurry that he doubted if he or any of his companions could find their way back to the treasure cache.

On the long train ride across Nebraska, young Goodale watched his chance and slipped off the train. He was never seen again, nor were any of the other bandits. The treasure, estimated to have a value of $240,000, has never been found. It rests somewhere out there in the Black Hills.

22.

OUTLAWS AND THEIR TREASURE

Outlaws, whether they were train robbers, bank robbers, highwaymen, rustlers, stage robbers, or just plain lawbreakers, all had the same problem of disposing of and protecting any surplus wealth they might accumulate through their unlawful activities. The simplest method was to hide it in some out-of-the-way place, mark the spot in a secret manner, and recover it when it was needed or when it was safe to do so.

If something happened—and it often did—to the members of the gang who knew where the treasure was buried, then the treasure became "lost." Frequently the hiding place of the treasure could not be found because of bad memories, changing landmarks, and many other reasons. In these cases the treasures are still there unless someone has stumbled upon them.

With modern police methods, organized gangs of outlaws have practically ceased to exist, although, of course, robberies and holdups still occur. But the old outlaws who defied the law and shot it out with the posses when

necessary are now a thing of the past. They have all gone to whatever reward was in store for them, but the stories of their buried loot still thrill the hunters of buried treasure.

The best known of the old Western outlaws, of course, was the Jesse James gang which terrorized many Western and Midwestern states and pulled off the first recorded train robbery in the United States. Down in the Wichita Mountains of southwestern Oklahoma many searches have been made for the $2,000,000 supposedly buried by the James gang along the old road from Fort Sill to the Keeche Hills. It is said that the gang robbed a rich Mexican transport and buried the loot that was too heavy to carry with them. If the James boys did bury treasure of such quantity, it could not have been accumulated from their numerous train and bank robberies, for records show that they probably secured less than $400,000 from their twenty-two known holdups.

Frank, the brother of Jesse James, often tried to find the loot he helped to bury, but during

89

the time he was a fugitive from the law, the country was divided up into farms and when he returned he failed to locate any of the markers. Later he bought a farm in the area and continued his search for the lost cache but it is believed that he never found it.

Several years ago a young man named Alvin Gilpin found a large stone in the mountainous region between Plainview and Hot Springs, Arkansas. On it was chiseled: "Frank-Jesse James $32,000 1877." Also there was pictured on the rock what appeared to be a code—a fork with three prongs, a bowie knife, and a cross. It was believed that the James gang used the stone as a marker for treasure buried in the vicinity at the time they held up the Hot Springs stage. The treasure was never found.

Kid Curry was the leader of a gang known as the Wild Bunch which operated in the mountain states from Montana to New Mexico. There were four Curry boys but the Kid's three brothers never lived to join his gang of outlaws. Johnnie was killed in a blazing gun battle with a man named Winters. Hank fell into an icy creek one night, caught pneumonia, and died with his boots beside the bed. Lonnie was killed by a deputy sheriff while trying to pull off a small holdup.

Kid Curry drifted around Montana until he was arrested one day by Pike Landusky for a minor infraction of the law. There had been bad blood between Curry and Landusky for some time, and the Kid vowed that Landusky, by arresting him, had dug his own grave. Landusky, himself an unsavory character, had somehow managed to get himself elected sheriff, and there was a strong sentiment in the Kid's favor.

A jury freed the Kid and he set out with just one thing on his mind—the killing of Pike Landusky. It happened on Christmas night. Landusky was leaning on the bar at Jake's Place in Fort Benton, when the Kid entered with the look of death on his face. Pike Landusky offered to shake hands, but the Kid's mind was made up and he refused. Landusky then hit him in the face, and the Kid went down bleeding at the mouth. When the Kid came up, his hand was on his Colt, and Landusky, carrying a new-fangled automatic, fired. It jammed, but the Kid didn't miss. Pike Landusky lay dead on the saw-dust floor.

When the Kid walked out of Jake's Place that Christmas night he knew he was now an outlaw, but he had one more score to settle. He rode to the cabin of the man Winters who had killed his brother, shouted to him, and, when he came to the door, shot him dead.

Attracting a number of infamous characters such as Flat Nose George, Bob Lee, and Harry Longabaugh, the Kid and the Wild Bunch ranged the Rockies, robbing banks and trains, rustling cattle, and holding up stages. In 1901 they held up a Great Northern passenger train near Malta, Montana, and got $80,000 which was cached somewhere near the scene of the holdup.

In the days before the railroads it was customary for traders and farmers to ship their merchandise to New Orleans on flatboats which merely drifted with the current down the Mississippi River. Reaching the New Orleans market, the traders would sell these boats and, pocketing the proceeds of their trip, they made their way back home afoot or on horseback.

The Natchez Trace was a wilderness road developed primarily for these returning boatmen. It ran northeastward from Natchez, crossing Mississippi and turning east into Tennessee for

a distance of some 300 miles to where it connected with the Tennessee River. Many of the Natchez Trace travelers carried considerable sums of money on their persons, and this fact, of course, attracted outlaws of all descriptions.

The first of the bandit gangs to see the possibilities of banditry on the Trace was Joseph Thompson Hare, a young tough from Pennsylvania. He grew rich off the Trace but was finally caught and hanged for robbing a mail coach in Maryland. His treasure is reportedly buried at several points along the Trace.

The two Harpe brothers, Micajah and Wiley, were perhaps the most notorious and bloodthirsty outlaws of their day. Along the Trace they left a trail of skeletons and a record for brutal killings seldom equaled in this country. Wiley, known as "Little Harpe," met the fate that he had exacted from so many of his victims. A companion shot him in the back, cut off his head, and carried it into Natchez where he claimed the reward offered for Wiley dead or alive.

Micajah, known as "Big Harpe," was finally caught by a group of enraged Kentuckians. They killed the outlaw, cut off his head, and hung it from a tree at a place now known as Harpe's Head in Kentucky. It is said that Big Harpe buried his loot near the place where he was killed but, although many people have searched for it, it has never been found.

Sam Mason was an ex-soldier turned outlaw. A strapping big Virginian, he had served in the Continental army with distinction. He had a system of spies and agents in Natchez and New Orleans who supplied him with tips when particularly well-heeled travelers left for the journey across the dangerous Trace.

Mason, too, was beheaded by his companions for the reward on his head. They slipped up behind him and crashed a tomahawk into his skull, cut off his head, rolled it in blue clay for preservation, and carried it to Natchez. One of the murderers was none other than Little Harpe!

Along the Mississippi, just outside Natchez, is a great cup-shaped hole in the ground known as the Devil's Punchbowl. In Sam Mason's day it was thickly overgrown with trees and brush and provided an ideal place of concealment. Here Mason made his headquarters and hiding place. Hundreds of people were certain that the outlaw had buried his treasure in the Devil's Punchbowl, and the area has been thoroughly dug over with picks and shovels. Early French and Spanish pirates are also said to have used the spot as a hiding place for their treasure.

The Mason gang is also said to have buried its treasure at a hideout near Rocky Springs, Mississippi, a small town along the old Trace about forty miles northeast of Natchez. Many people have searched for the Mason treasure, but it is believed that none of it has ever been found.

John Murrell was one of the last of the famous Trace outlaws. Aside from common outlawry, his forte was stealing Negro slaves and selling them back to their owners as "captured runaways." He was eventually captured through the clever work of a young man named Virgil Stewart who set out to avenge the theft of slaves from his father. Murrell was the only Trace outlaw to die a natural death. Tuberculosis, contracted during his many years in prison, finally ended his bloody career.

Murrell made his headquarters at a stone house which he built about three miles outside the little town of Denmark, Tennessee. It still stands, and it is claimed that he buried near his home an estimated million dollars in gold.

Butch Cassidy was one of the most unique outlaws the West has ever known. A big, good-natured fellow who loved fun and excitement, the only man he ever killed in his long career of holdups and robberies was himself!

Cassidy, whose real name was George Leroy Parker, was the son of a Mormon rancher in Utah. He got into a boyish fight with another lad over a schoolgirl. Thinking he had killed the lad, Cassidy ran away and eventually joined up with the Hole-in-the-Wall gang, a bunch of bandits operating out of Wyoming.

Kid Curry eventually took the Hole-in-the-Wall gang into his Wild Bunch and, with his sudden demise, Cassidy inherited the leadership of the gang which ranged all the way from Montana down to the Mexican border.

Cassidy was a perfectionist. He believed that a well-planned robbery could be pulled off without killing anyone and he proved this more than once. Deciding to hold up the San Miguel Valley Bank at Telluride, Colorado, Butch spent weeks preparing for the bloodless robbery. He rode a very fine horse—for which he had paid a fancy price because he didn't believe in stealing horses. The animal was trained to perfection, for this was part of the plan.

Across the street from the bank was a hitching rack. Cassidy trained his horse to stand untied at the rack until he whistled from across the street. Then the animal would back across to him and come to a stop directly in front of the bank. Cassidy, with a running start, would vault onto the horse from behind and the animal would gallop down the street at top speed.

For two weeks the cowboy and the horse went through the act in front of the bank until there was never a hitch in their performance. At first the natives thought the cowboy was a bit goofy, but finally they paid no attention to him. Then one day Cassidy drifted into the bank, drew his two six-shooters, and commanded the surprised teller to throw all the cash into the sack that he pushed through the cage.

Grabbing the sack, Cassidy gave a loud whistle and dashed for the door just as his trained horse backed into position. With a leap he was aboard and the horse took off at full gallop! For his two week's work he received $30,000—and nobody had been hurt!

Cassidy's interests finally turned to train-robbing, and he became such a pest to the Union Pacific that the railroad officials offered to put him on the payroll if he would agree to leave their trains alone. Cassidy accepted but soon tired of the dull life of a train guard and returned to the Wild Bunch.

Around 1900 Western sheriffs were beginning to break up the Wild Bunch, and Cassidy decided that the good old days were about to end. He and Harry Longabaugh went to South America and renewed their outlaw activities. Suspected of rustling cattle, the two Americans were surrounded by a group of soldiers near the Argentine-Chile border in 1904. During the fight Longabaugh was killed. Cassidy fought alone throughout the night. Early in the morning he had but one bullet left and he sent it crashing through his own head—the only man he ever killed!

Cassidy's treasure is reputedly buried at many points in the mountain states, but it is fairly certain that he cached $70,000 when hard-pressed by a posse in the Wind River Mountains area of western Wyoming.

Every section of the United States has had its outlaws and each gang has left its legend of buried treasure. There was Joaquín Murietta and Tiburcio Vásquez in California, whose treasure is reportedly buried in a dozen different places. Nebraska had its Pony Gang, and Colorado was ravaged by the Reynolds Gang who supposedly buried treasure on Spanish Peaks. Rube Burrows and the Copeland Gang ranged over Mississippi, and the Plummer Gang, operating as officers of the law in Montana, held up many a treasure-laden stage. The Pine Robbers in New Jersey, the Loomis Gang in New York, and the Doane Gang in Pennsylvania all left records of buried treasure.

Indiana had its Reno Gang, Wisconsin had the Maxwell Gang, while Pierre Rambeau operated in Louisiana. In the midwestern states the Daltons, the Doolins, Al Jennings, and the Buck Gang kept the railroads and the banks worried. Sam Bass, Blackjack Ketchum, and a host of others terrorized the Southwest, and Florida had its Ed Watson Gang and the Ashleys. In modern times there was John Dillinger whose treasure is buried somewhere near Rhinelander, Wisconsin, and the Touhy Gang of Chicago who are thought to have buried treasure near Newport, Tennessee.

"Hands up!" and "Throw down that box!" were well-known commands in the days of the old West. It meant that somebody had treasure and somebody else wanted it! A great deal of the gold exchanging hands at the point of a gun found its way into the ground—and there it waits for a finder.

23.

THE BURIED TREASURE OF SKELETON CANYON

Now AND THEN a human bone is picked up at the entrance to Skeleton Canyon in southeastern Arizona—a grisly reminder of that day in 1882 when Curly Bill Brocius and a gang of outlaws planned to waylay a Mexican smuggling train and capture a cool three million dollars in treasure.

This section of Arizona is a land of wild and rugged mountains, some rising abruptly from the desert, while others, massed against each other, appear like dark storm clouds on the distant horizon. It is a land of broad valleys and strange, deceptive distances. The high degree of visibility is the subject of many local stories such as the one about the cowboy who swore he saw a lady wink at him a mile away.

Skeleton Canyon winds through the wildest part of the Peloncillo Mountains from Las Animas Valley in New Mexico to San Bernardino Valley in Arizona. Now a place of peace and solitude, its stillness broken only by the occasional bawls of cattle or by the night howls of prowling coyotes, it was the scene many years ago of two brutal battles between outlaws and smugglers.

Curly Bill Brocius was a bronzed, blue-eyed giant of a man with dark kinky hair. He always wore high-heeled, fancy-stitched boots, a wide-brimmed white sombrero, and two criss-crossed gun belts to hold his twin forty-fours. He was a discriminating bandit, boasting that he robbed only the wealthy, but his special delight was the caravans of Mexican smugglers which made frequent trips between Old Mexico and Tucson or Phoenix.

A rustler, too, Curly Bill showed a marked preference for Mexican cattle, and his name was prominent in a number of hot-worded diplomatic notes exchanged by the two countries.

Headquarters for Curly Bill and his gang of bandits and rustlers was the small town of Galeyville located in a well-watered canyon of the Chiricahua Mountains. Far from the sheriff's office and almost inaccessible from the Tombstone side, Galeyville was a resort for badmen of all kinds, and Curly Bill was its undisputed master.

One day in 1882 word reached Curly Bill that Mexican smugglers planned to bring into Arizona a cargo that would far surpass in value anything previously handled. Curly Bill decided pronto to have that treasure! He immediately sent a henchman, Jim Hughes, to Sonora to scout the land and get the details.

Hughes, a swarthy half-Mexican who spoke perfect Spanish, had no trouble making friends in Mexico, and before long the smugglers were drinking tequila toasts to their new member.

Many tequilas later, Hughes learned that the smugglers would pass through Skeleton Canyon in August and that the cargo would, indeed, be the most valuable ever taken out of Mexico—the loot accumulated from scores of Mexican robberies.

Bursting with the good news, Hughes slipped away and hurried back to Galeyville to report to Curly Bill. The outlaw leader was away on a private mission, however, and nobody seemed to know when he would return. This gave Hughes time to think, and the more he thought about that rich treasure coming across the Peloncillos, the more he was inclined to double-cross Curly Bill and pull the job himself. It was dangerous, but it was worth the try.

Recruiting Zwing Hunt, a toughened old mule-skinner who aspired to be a big-shot outlaw, a nineteen-year-old desperado named Billy Grounds, and five other less prominent residents of Galeyville, Hughes divulged his plan and swore them all to secrecy. They all were with him.

One starry night early in August the eight outlaws sneaked out of Galeyville, rode across San Simon Valley, and entered Skeleton Canyon. There they hid in the rocks forming the canyon wall.

Next morning the Mexican pack train of fifteen men and twice as many mules came winding up the trail across the Peloncillos and down into the canyon. Black eyes under peaked sombreros craftily scanned the cliffs for signs of danger as they passed through Devil's Kitchen. Guns were cocked and ready.

Near the canyon's entrance the smugglers stopped for a lunch and siesta before tackling the long hot stretch across San Simon Valley. Guards were hurriedly posted up and down the canyon, and the men stretched out in the grass in the shade of an oak tree while the tired mules grazed lazily near by.

Suddenly there came a fusillade of rifle fire from the rocky walls above the canyon floor, and the area exploded in a roar of crashing echoes. Three Mexicans lay dead and the others were seized with panic. The camp sprang into a wildly confused tangle of shouting, running men, rearing horses, and stampeding mules.

The surviving smugglers jumped on their ponies and galloped down the canyon, bullets whistling after them. The heavily laden mules, plunging and kicking in fright, scattered in all directions, spilling the rich contents of their packs.

Out of the ambush rode the outlaws in hot pursuit of the treasure, and the canyon shook with gunfire until the last mule was run down and killed.

The battle over, the bandits were faced with the problem of what to do with the loot. Dead men and mules lay scattered in the canyon and far out into the valley. Two men started digging a huge hole in the ground beneath the oak tree while the others collected the scattered treasure.

This is a partial inventory of the treasure as revealed later by one of the bandits on his death bed: a cigar box full of diamonds worth a million dollars, stolen from a bank vault in Monterrey, Mexico; thirty-nine bars of gold bullion valued at $600,000; scores of silver ingots; 90,-000 Mexican gold dollars; countless sacks of gold and silver coins; two life-sized statues of pure gold which once adorned sanctuary niches in a Mexican cathedral.

The treasure buried temporarily, Hughes led

the gang back to Galeyville. Death was the penalty for the man who as much as breathed any information regarding the robbery. A few days later Hughes pulled the second double-cross. He instructed Zwing Hunt and Billy Grounds, his two closest companions, to move the treasure to a safer and permanent hiding place. The two men agreed with him that there was no point—nor profit—in cutting in the five other robbers!

Hunt and Grounds hired an old Mexican teamster with a four-horse wagon. The treasure was dug up and removed to a secret hiding place with the aged Mexican doing most of the work for he was promised a liberal percentage of the treasure for his efforts. But it wasn't the intention of the two outlaws to share with the Mexican nor to have him live to tell the story. When the work was almost completed, the Mexican was killed and tossed into the hole. His horses were then killed, and the wagon was burned near the spot.

Hughes waited in Galeyville for the return of his companions, but days passed and finally he realized the awful truth—he, too, had been

double-crossed. Jim Hughes resolved to regain that treasure if possible. Some place, sometime, he would encounter Zwing Hunt and Billy Grounds, and there would be the very devil to pay.

Hunt and Grounds were hiding out on the Chandler Ranch near the little cowtown of Charleston, waiting for things to cool down when they were surprised by Deputy Sheriff Healey. Suspected of killing the son of a prominent local judge in a holdup, they had been on the sheriff's wanted list for several weeks. Minutes after Healey found the two outlaws, the smell of powder was still in the air when this message was sent to the sheriff at Tombstone: "Send the coroner to Jack Chandler's ranch. One of our men dead. Billy Grounds dying. Also Zwing Hunt. Jack Young shot through thigh. I got creased in the neck."

Young Billy Grounds lived until the following morning, and Hunt, shot through both lungs, was taken to Tombstone in a wagon and placed in the hospital under armed guard.

As soon as Jim Hughes learned of Hunt's capture he raced to the hospital, determined to find out where the treasure was hidden before the wounded outlaw died. But Zwing Hunt had remarkable recuperative power—and some friends. When Hughes arrived at the hospital, Hunt was gone—whisked out a back door and carried away in a wagon, presumably by a relative.

Sometime later a Hugh Hunt appeared in Tombstone and announced that Zwing Hunt had been killed by Indians as he was eating breakfast one morning in the Swisshelm Mountains. Skeptics were taken to the spot where Zwing was supposed to be buried and, sure enough, there was a fresh grave. This should have ended the treasure story since Zwing Hunt was the last remaining person to know the burial place of the treasure, but this same Zwing Hunt miraculously turned up later in his old home town of San Antonio, Texas.

Presumably Hugh Hunt assisted Zwing in getting to Mexico where he remained in hiding for several years, not daring to go back to Arizona for the treasure and never fully recovered from his wounds. Finally he went to San Antonio to seek a doctor. The doctor told Zwing that he had not long to live. Gangrene had set in.

Zwing called Hugh to his side and related the story of the buried treasure, describing in detail the landmarks that would lead to the cache. Here are the directions as related by the dying outlaw: *The treasure is buried at the foot of Davis Mountain. To the east stretches open rolling plains, and from the top of the peak you can see a portion of western New Mexico. One and one-half miles west of the peak is a canyon of many curves, hemmed in on one side by wooded hills and on the other by a sheer rock precipice. Through the canyon flows a small stream with a ten-foot waterfall. Near the waterfalls are two springs about a mile apart. One spring is called "Silver Spring," the other is called "Gum Spring." About halfway between the two springs, but slightly closer to Silver Spring, is the treasure cache. Above the treasure is a square stone. On the east side of the stone are chiseled two crosses, one above the other.*

Find this spot and you will be standing directly over three million dollars in treasure! The description is of the upper reaches of Skeleton Canyon, but the landmarks mentioned by Zwing Hunt are baffling. There is no Davis Mountain in the vicinity! Was Zwing Hunt double-crossing the man who saved him from sure death at the hands of Jim Hughes?

The details of this story are mainly authentic, but the facts are puzzling. The search goes on, however, for the treasure of Skeleton Canyon!

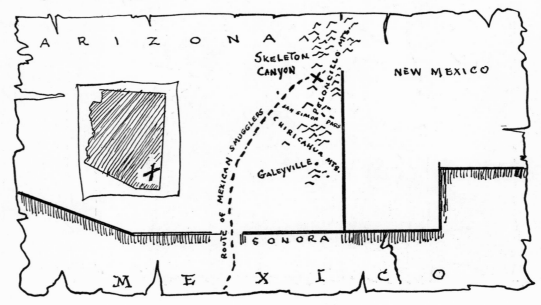

24.

THE BURIED TREASURE OF COLOSSAL CAVE

THOUSANDS OF YEARS AGO a great river rushed out of the side of Rincon Mountain, 17 miles east of Tucson, Arizona, and poured down the mountain. Suddenly this mysterious river dried up leaving the magnificent caverns under Rincon Mountain known today as Colossal Cave.

Colossal Cave is actually a series of exquisite and spectacular limestone passages, rooms and caverns. The cave is always dry and the air is always fresh. In both winter and summer the temperature never varies from a constant 72 degrees—a perfect setting for a treasure story.

So far as is known Colossal Cave was unknown to white men until 1884 when Sheriff Bob Leatherwood of Tucson chased a band of train robbers into "the hole in the ground." In some manner known only to themselves the bandits had learned that a certain Southern Pacific Railroad train would be carrying a large consignment of gold for the railroad's payroll and for the troops stationed at old Fort Lowell.

The bandits selected the drowsy little town of Pantano as the site of the robbery. It was lo-

cated in rugged desert country and close to the mountains that would cover their escape. As the train was about to pull out of the little desert station, four men suddenly appeared from the shadows, overpowered the two Wells, Fargo guards, quickly seized the gold—$62,000 in all—and galloped rapidly away. It all happened with such precision and determination that the train was about to pull out before the open-mouthed station agent realized that a holdup had taken place.

The train raced into Tucson and the alarm was spread. Sheriff Leatherwood and a couple of tough Wells, Fargo agents had no difficulty in forming a posse of pay-hungry railroad workers, angry citizens, and armed soldiers. In a few hours the posse was riding out of Tucson in a cloud of dust, headed for Pantano and the bandit trail.

From the scene of the robbery the four bandits were trailed some eight or nine miles across the desert floor along the foothills of the Rincon Mountains. The trail ended at the

Rancho del Lago, owned by a colored man named Crane.

Crane denied vigorously that any strangers had been there, but Sheriff Leatherwood demanded an explanation of the four well-lathered horses in the corral. "My horses," said Crane. "Stolen horses, then," replied the sheriff. "That isn't your brand!"

The frightened Negro finally broke down and admitted that four strange men had ridden up to the ranch and forced him to exchange mounts with them. They had threatened him with death if he breathed a word of it to anybody. Where had they gone? Why, they rode off toward that hole in the ground up on the side of Rincon Mountain!

There was little doubt that these four men were the bandits. The posse rode off and soon arrived at an unimpressive-looking hole which appeared to be the entrance to a small cave. Hidden in the near-by brush were the four horses belonging to Crane. Sheriff Leatherwood was certain that the bandits had gone into the cave—and were trapped.

A few of the braver members of the posse ventured into the narrow opening, which sloped abruptly downward and plunged into utter blackness. They had not gone more than a few feet when a volley of gun shots sent them scrambling for the entrance. It was one of the shortest and strangest gun fights in Western history with the bark of six-guns echoing through the cavern like thunder and bullets ricocheting from stalactite to stalagmite. This was more than the posse had bargained for. They gathered outside and took council.

Finally it was Sheriff Leatherwood's decision to capture the bandits in a less hazardous manner. The cave, he reasoned, had but one entrance—and that was also the exit. Eventually the bandits would have to emerge. What could be simpler than waiting for them? A camp was hurriedly established and a party was sent to Tucson to bring supplies.

Two long weeks passed, and the sheriff and his party began to tire of poker. Not a sign of the bandits had as much as broken the monotony. Now it was time to do something about the situation. A large pile of branches and brush was placed in the mouth of the cave and set afire. This would surely smoke the orneriest critter out, assured the sheriff. Not a thing happened.

The posse was about to give up and Leatherwood was trying to organize another group to enter the cave when a cowboy rode in from Willcox with startling news. There were four strangers in Willcox who were boasting loudly between drinks that they had put a good one over on the sheriff! Bob Leatherwood began to smell a rat. Could they be the bandits? Could the cave have a second entrance?

Leaving part of the posse on guard at the cave entrance, the sheriff set out for Willcox and a personal investigation. He had no trouble locating the strangers. With an armed force to back him up, the sheriff approached the strangers and ordered them to throw up their hands. The bandits replied by drawing their guns and opening fire. The battle was short and decisive. After the smoke had cleared away, Sheriff Leatherwood had three dead bandits and a wounded prisoner on his hands. Thanks to the inebriated condition of the strangers, not one of the sheriff's party was injured.

The captured bandit revealed just what the

sheriff had expected. They had emerged from the cave several days ago through another entrance located not far from the posse's camp. The robber admitted that the entire amount taken from the train was hidden in the cave, but refused to reveal its hiding place. "You can hang me first," he said. "I'll never tell."

The prisoner wasn't hanged, however, but was sentenced to twenty-eight years in the Territorial Prison in Yuma, refusing a shorter term offered in exchange for revealing the hiding place of the treasure.

During the bandit's imprisonment, Wells, Fargo agents tried by every known means to force the secret from him. He changed his story slightly and said that he had been standing guard at the entrance to the cave when the treasure was buried. This the agents would not believe, but no amount of duress would produce any other story.

Following the slaying of the bandits, Wells, Fargo kept a searching party in Colossal Cave for almost three months, but it was a hopeless task for the cave turned out to be a maze of passages, bottomless pits, and caverns which haven't been fully explored to this day!

Wells, Fargo, in its dogged way, saw to it that the prisoner served his full term, and when his release finally came in 1912, two Wells, Fargo agents were lurking in Yuma to take up his trail.

The ex-prisoner, apparently aware of the agents following him, went to Tucson where he remained a couple of weeks. The agents became careless, and the man suddenly slipped quietly out of town. Certain that the ex-prisoner had headed for Colossal Cave to recover the treasure, the agents secured fast horses and lost no time in getting to the cave, but it was too late. If the ex-bandit had visited the cave he had covered his tracks well. Not a trace of him could be found.

Several years later an exploration party found several empty money sacks in a small room that contains the only loose earth in the cave. It was assumed that this had been the burial room of the treasure and that searching parties must have crossed over it many times in their fruitless search for the missing $62,000.

The surviving bandit was never seen to emerge from the cave nor was he ever again seen by anyone who could identify him after his disappearance from Tucson. This has led to the almost positive belief that the ex-convict recovered the treasure, but never left the cave with it. The theory is that he attempted to leave the cave by the little-known exit and either fell to his death in one of the many dark pits or became lost and starved to death. It would be extremely easy to do in Colossal Cave. Whatever his fate, the $62,000 stolen at Pantano is still believed to be buried somewhere in the jet black interior of the cavern.

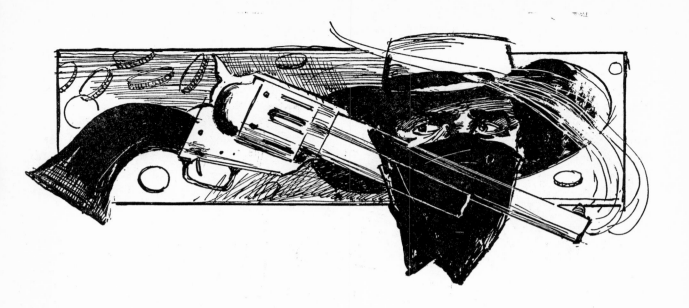

25.

THE GREAT TRAIN ROBBERY TREASURE

SEVEN OUTLAWS, all armed with pistols, lay in hiding near the railroad tracks at Marshfield, Indiana, May 22, 1868. Puffing in from the south, drawn by a wood-burning locomotive that lurched and tugged, its wide stack belching black smoke and tongues of red flame, came the passenger train of the Jefferson, Madison and Indianapolis line, due at Indianapolis at two-forty Saturday.

Marshfield was a wood-and-water stop, and the only people waiting for the train were the outlaws, who were scattered about in strategic positions. Two of them were behind the pile of corded wood where the engine would stop. Two were concealed behind trees at both sides of the track, and another, probably Frank Reno himself, had a lookout post from which he could observe the entire scene.

As the train squealed to a stop, the engineer climbed down carrying his oil can and was immediately knocked unconscious with a blow from a pistol butt. At the same moment two outlaws jumped into the cab and overpowered the fireman, while two others darted to the couplings behind the Adams Express car, which was next to the tender.

From one of the passenger coaches the conductor, John Whedon, stepped down and saw the men at the couplings. He drew a pistol and fired. A bullet from a bandit gun whizzed past his ear. He fired two more shots and a return bullet cut through his coat. That was enough. He sprang aboard the coach, out of range.

All seven bandits now jammed into the tiny cab, where one of them, probably Charles Anderson, who knew how to operate the engine, released the brakes and opened the throttle. The passenger cars were left behind while the locomotive and express car gathered speed and plunged northward, covering twenty miles in a little more than twenty minutes. Three or four miles south of Seymour, where the express car was to be robbed, the train ground to a stop.

Both doors of the express car were securely locked inside, but the outlaws quickly smashed in the side door and found only one guard inside, Thomas Harkins. He was knocked out, bound, robbed of his keys, and then thrown from the car as the engine started again.

After the keys failed to open the two money safes containing $80,000, Charlie Anderson, an experienced safecracker, went to work on them.

Finally, with the money in their hands, the outlaws moved a little closer to Seymour and abandoned the train. They now set out afoot to the little village of Rockford the home town of the Reno outfit, about two miles north of Seymour. Somewhere between Seymour and Rockford the loot was buried in a woods so that it would not be found on them if they were captured.

The southern part of Indiana had been terrorized by the Reno boys for a couple of years. They were arrested from time to time but never convicted, and there was angry talk that they had political connections.

There were five Reno brothers—Frank, Simeon, William, John, and Clinton. At the time of the robbery, John was serving a prison sentence in Missouri. Clint, known as the "honest Reno boy," took no part in the gang's activities. A sister, Laura, often assisted the gang in a minor way, but on the night of the train holdup she was in Ohio. This involved three of the Renos in the Marshfield robbery.

Immediately after the holdup strong public determination arose to clean the gang out once and for all. A vigilante committee was formed and to show that it meant business, seven hoodlums were hanged during the next few months. Each member of the vigilantes wore a red velvet mask.

Meantime the Reno gang took the hint and left the country, with the Pinkertons close on their trail. Frank, William, and Simeon, together with Charlie Anderson, hit the road for Canada where they were finally found and arrested. Anderson claimed to be a British citizen, and the Canadian authorities were reluctant to let any of the four be extradited. Finally Canada permitted the prisoners to be taken back to Indiana on the assurance that the men would be given adequate protection from the vigilantes and be granted a fair trial. They got neither.

For safekeeping the prisoners were taken to New Albany, just across the Ohio River from Louisville, and locked up in the new jail. It had steel cells and the town was very proud of it.

On the night of December 14 a mystery train consisting of a locomotive and one passenger coach pulled into New Albany between three

and four o'clock in the morning when the town was sound asleep. It came to a stop at Pearl Street, and about seventy-five men all wearing red masks stepped out. They were armed with guns, clubs, ropes, and even slingshots!

As the mob marched to the jail, patrols were posted to assure that there would be no interference with their retreat. Lookouts were posted outside the jail. Inside the jail office, they found one lone guard, who was immediately over-powered and bound to a chair. Two more guards in the jail yard were quickly disposed of.

A group of men went to the room occupied by the sheriff and his wife. The surprised sheriff came to the door in his undershirt and drawers. "Hand over the keys or we'll shoot," ordered the masked men.

"Go ahead and shoot!" said the sheriff, slamming the door and making for an open window. He reached the jail yard and ran into a dozen masked men with drawn pistols. He was tied up and placed under guard.

The keys were finally located, and the mob went to the cell block where they encountered another guard. He threatened to shoot but de-cided against it when told that he, too, would be hanged if he interfered.

The four hangings took only a few minutes, as one by one, the prisoners were strung up from the steel framework of the cell block. Each man was offered a chance for his life if he would agree to lead the party to the buried $80,000. Each in turn refused.

This left three of the original seven bandits at large. Not one of them was ever seen again, and it was believed that the hanged men had done away with their partners before fleeing to Canada so that they would not recover the treasure for themselves. As far as known the express-car treasure is still buried where the Reno boys placed it that night in 1868. Perhaps one day a plow will turn it up.

26.

HENRY GORDIER'S LOST TREASURE

HENRY GORDIER was murdered by a group of men seeking his buried treasure. They didn't find it, nor has anyone else unless the secret has been well kept. It was buried on his ranch on Baxter Creek, not far from the town of Janesville, California, on the north side of Honey Lake.

Gordier and Isaac Coulthurst were prospecting partners in the California diggings. Unlike most shiftless miners, Gordier and Coulthurst stuck with a good strike when they found one. They worked hard and both men amassed a considerable fortune in gold dust and nuggets. Tiring of the mines, Gordier purchased a ranch on Baxter Creek and prepared to take things easier. He had heard that the Mormons of Carson Valley were selling their stock and returning to Salt Lake City, and their ranch was just what he was looking for.

In the fall of 1857 he had accumulated quite a herd of Durham cattle, the best in the valley, and he was known as a man of wealth and in-

tegrity. Even after outfitting and stocking his ranch, there was plenty of gold left over. He followed the custom and buried it somewhere on his property.

One day in early March 1858, Sol Perrin, who lived near the northeast corner of Honey Lake, noticed a lone rider approaching on the road to Gordier's ranch. As the man drew nearer, Perrin recognized him as Lucky Bill Thorrington, a gambler he had once known at Placerville. He called out and Thorrington stopped for a chat. The conversation finally drifted around to Gordier's cattle, and the gambler said that he was headed up the valley to try to buy some of the fine Durham stock.

"Well, good luck," said Perrin, "but I don't think Henry'll sell. He's mighty proud of those critters." Thorrington rode away.

William B. Thorrington was a native of New York. He had come to California in 1850 and established himself as a gambler at Placerville, although there were few mining camps where his 200-pound, six-foot figure and jet black curly hair wasn't known. His brilliant dark eyes reflected great humor and he had the faculty of making an unhappy man forget his losses at faro. In a rich baritone voice he could quote the Bible with deep feeling or order the execution of a man.

After a trip to Michigan Lucky Bill came west again and established himself in Genoa in Carson Valley. He owned shares in the Carson toll road, a gambling house, and several other less legitimate enterprises. It was common knowledge that Lucky Bill was the man to see if you were a rustler or a highwayman and needed a refuge from the law. That is, if you could pay Lucky Bill's exorbitant price. Life and property in Carson Valley had no more security than Lucky Bill saw fit to give.

It so happened that Sol Perrin saw Thorrington return from Gordier's ranch on the following day. Again he talked to the big gambler and asked if he had purchased the Durhams. Thorrington replied that the deal looked pretty good.

The transaction wasn't completed, it was true, but he had engaged some friends to handle the matter for him. "Sure surprised," said Perrin, "Henry was mighty proud of those critters."

Later in the month, Perrin and other neighbors were surprised to hear that Henry Gordier had left the country and that a man named Asa Snow had moved into his house. Who was Asa Snow? Somebody recalled that he had lived in a cabin up on Lassen Creek with two other men, a William Combs and John Mullen.

All three men had kept quietly to themselves. Rumor had it that Mullen was running a few cattle on the place and had a weakness for picking up stray calves. It was even more vaguely rumored that Snow had once killed a man and was lying low. Of Combs, not much was known, except that he worked a few placers near by.

Neighbors thought it was time to meet Asa Snow. They rode over and got right to the point —where was Henry Gordier? Snow had immediate answers. Gordier had sold the ranch and stock to John Mullen and was right now in Genoa with Mullen and William Combs closing the deal. Snow had been hired as caretaker until Mullen returned and took over the property.

"Sounds damn queer to me," said Perrin. "That hain't like Henry Gordier, going away and sayin' nuthin' to nobody!" The others agreed with him.

It was April when Mullen and Combs returned from Genoa. They reported that Gordier, after closing the deal in Genoa, had met an old shipmate there and had suddenly left town, intending to return to his native France.

Some time after the mysterious disappearance of Henry Gordier, one of the settlers of Honey Valley received a letter from Gordier's brother in Plumas County. He had heard the news of his brother's departure and he did not believe a word of it. His brother, he declared, would not leave the country without seeing him. This added fuel to the growing suspicions.

During the last days of April there was a dance at Arnold's Hotel in Genoa in celebration of the defeat of a band of Indian cattle thieves. Everyone of importance attended and the main topic of conversation was the disappearance of Henry Gordier. A rancher named Charles Adams wondered if an incident that he recalled might not have had some connection with the mystery. On March 15, he said, he had lost eight head of cattle. A posse was organized to search for the missing cattle and bring the rustlers to justice. One night it was camped on the north bank of Willow Creek, close by Gordier's ranch. At dusk the campers heard the crack of a single shot from across the creek and saw the flicker of a distant fire. At first they had thought it to be a signal from reinforcements they expected, or perhaps the night bivouac of a lone traveler. By morning the incident was forgotten.

When this news broke, a party was immediately organized to investigate. On the banks of Willow Creek opposite the spot where the Adams party had camped, they found ashes containing some metal buttons, traces of dried blood, and tracks leading down to a deep pothole in the river. One of the men stripped and dived into the hole, but the water was too cold and he had to give up without finding anything. Samples of the dried blood were taken to a doctor in Genoa who pronounced it human blood.

A second search party was organized and, working from a raft with long poles, fished up a body from the pothole. It was, as everyone suspected, the body of Henry Gordier. His legs had been jacknifed around a large stone and tightly bound. A single bullet hole was found in the back of his head.

The finding of Gordier's body touched off an explosion. A jury immediately named Mullen and Combs as the murderers and implicated Snow and Thorrington as accomplices in the plot to secure Gordier's ranch, stock, and treasure. The hunt for the killers was on.

Snow was found on a near-by ranch. At the approach of the posse he drew his gun, but was overpowered. He defiantly denied any knowledge of the murder, even when taken to a tall pine tree and threatened with hanging. He continued to hurl abuse at his captors. Twice he was hauled up and twice let down. On the third hoist the committee misjudged their timing. Snow was dead.

At this time a man named Rough Elliott stepped up and offered to help find Mullen and Combs. He had, he stated, lived for a short time with the two men in the cabin on Lassen Creek. Combs's real name, he asserted, was William Combs Edwards, and he was wanted for the murder of a postmaster in Merced County. There was a $1500 reward for his capture.

A floater from the diggings, Elliott enjoyed just about bottom place on the social ladder at Genoa—the kind of a character who might be able to put the finger on Lucky Bill Thorrington. The posse accepted his services.

Elliott's approach to Thorrington must have been convincing, for Lucky Bill was not a man easily taken in. Before long Elliott was one of the backroom boys at Thorrington's establishment and was piecing together valuable information of the gambler's diversified activities.

Not fully confident that Elliott was on the level, the posse set another trap to ensnare the gambler of Genoa. A fast and well-known mare named Bald Hornet was given to Junius Brutus Gilpin, who furtively rode it into Genoa and reported to Lucky Bill that he had stolen it. The gambler was taken in and, for a price, offered Gilpin a hiding place until things blew over.

Word was now received from Elliott that Mullen and Edwards were leaving the area over a certain road. The posse organized to intercept the two fleeing killers. When it arrived at the designated spot, Edwards was alone, riding Bald Hornet. After a running exchange of shots the horse was wounded, but Edwards took to the hills on foot and escaped.

Through the spying of Elliott and Gilpin, sufficient evidence was now at hand to justify the arrest of Lucky Bill. He and his seventeen-year-old son, Jerome, were taken without resistance at the Thorrington house in Genoa and escorted to a ranch on Clear Creek for safekeeping. Of course, Lucky Bill denied any knowledge of the crime, but Jerome let it slip that he knew where Edwards was hiding. The posse offered Jerome his freedom if he would lure Edwards to the Thorrington ranch. The frightened lad agreed.

At midnight two days later Jerome and Edwards approached the Thorrington cabin. In-side the door stood three armed members of the posse. Edwards, heavily armed, suspected a trap and waited outside while Jerome entered the house. "All's well," called Jerome. "Come on in!" As Edwards entered the door he was promptly knocked down, disarmed, and tied up.

A special jury of eighteen men tried Edwards and Thorrington. Edwards turned prosecution witness and confessed the crime. He and Mullen, he related, had tricked Gordier into going down to the banks of Willow Creek to see a sick cow. Here they overpowered him but were unsuccessful in forcing him to tell where his gold was. Mullen shot him in the head, and his body was weighted and thrown into the pothole.

The jury's verdict was death by hanging for both men. Edwards at his hanging on June 23 made a last-minute speech clearing Snow of any part in Gordier's murder. Lucky Bill, cool and joking to the last, was hanged from a tree on his own ranch. Mullen was never heard of again.

As a partial reward for his part in trapping Lucky Bill, Rough Elliott was given Bald Hornet. His stature in the community had been increased vastly by his part in solving the crime.

Many parties searched for the gold buried by Henry Gordier, and in 1877 a woman found a small cache of several nuggets in the vicinity of the cabin, but everyone is certain that the main treasure is still where Henry Gordier buried it.

27.

MAXIMILIAN'S BURIED TREASURE

CASTLE GAP, in the King Mountains, is one of the gateways to western Texas. Through the narrow canyon ran the southern route of the gold seekers of '49, and later the towering walls echoed to the rumble of the Butterfield stagecoaches. Pack trains clattered through the Gap behind patient bell mares, and freight wagons wore deep ruts in the canyon floor which may be seen to this day.

A great deal of Western history was written around Castle Gap. Indians waylaid the lumbering wagon trains, and outlaws lurked in hiding to pounce upon the stages, but one of the strangest stories of the Gap concerns fifteen *carreta* loads of treasure buried in the vicinity. A *carreta* is a crude two-wheeled Mexican cart pulled by oxen and has been used throughout the Southwest for hundreds of years.

When the United States was engaged in the Civil War, Napoleon III of France took advantage of the situation to place the Austrian archduke, Maximilian, on the throne of Mexico, along with his Empress, Carlotta.

The Maximilian rule was doomed from the start as Mexican patriots planned the day when they would be strong enough to throw the foreigners out. Sensing the impending disaster, Maximilian sent his wife to Europe to secure military help with which to hold his throne. Empress Carlotta went mad and never returned. It was just as well. Her fate in Mexico would have been the firing squad beside her husband.

When Emperor Maximilian came to Mexico, he brought with him a great personal fortune and he amassed more during the three years he clung precariously to the Mexican throne. Of that vast fortune there remain today at Chapultepec Castle in Mexico City a few jewels and some pieces of gold and silver plate. What became of the rest of it? Here is the story frequently told throughout the Southwest.

In 1866, nearly a year before Maximilian's empire fell and he was executed at Cerro de las Campanas, the Emperor was concerned with getting his personal treasure out of Mexico before he would himself have to flee in the night.

111

One day fifteen heavily loaded *carretas* left the castle and headed north. The *carretas* were carefully covered with canvas, even though, according to the four Austrians in charge, they held nothing more precious than barrels of flour.

Inside the barrels—and there were perhaps forty or fifty of them—were the treasures of Emperor Maximilian—coins, gold and silver plate and ornaments, chests of jewels, and gold and silver bullion, all carefully packed and resting underneath a layer of flour!

The four Austrians, close friends of the Emperor, rode fine horses. In charge of each of the fifteen teams of oxen was a Mexican peon, who knew nothing of the valuable cargo they were hauling. After several days of forced marching the caravan safely reached Presidio del Norte (El Paso) and crossed to Texas soil. The Austrians were greatly relieved to be out of Mexico and felt that the greatest danger was now over. It was only beginning, however. Being close to the border, the area was full of dangerous men —Indians, outlaws, highwaymen, and adventurers of all types.

At Presidio del Norte the caravan paused for a few days' rest and the Austrians met six ex-Confederate soldiers from Missouri, who, distrustful of their fate at the hands of the carpetbaggers from the North, were fleeing to Mexico. They had just come over the road from San Antonio and reported that every mile of it was infested with hostile Indians and badmen.

The Austrians confided that they had a very valuable load of flour which they must deliver in San Antonio without further delay. Would the six Missourians consider guiding the caravan to San Antonio and act as a guard? There would be a handsome reward if the trip across the plains was made in safety.

The ex-soldiers, glad to have the opportunity to replenish their dwindling funds, accepted the offer and guaranteed safe conduct for the *carreta* train, although it hardly seemed as though a cargo of flour required a military escort!

Everything went smoothly for the first few days, but the close manner in which the Austrians guarded the *carretas* at night aroused the curiosity of the Missourians. "Something in those carts besides flour!" said one. They determined to find out for themselves.

One night when the caravan was drawn up at a camp site near the Pecos River, the ex-soldiers put their plan into action. While five of the men lured the guards away from the *carretas* temporarily, the sixth lifted the canvas on some of the carts and pried open a few of the barrels enough to find out whether the flour was merely a ruse. They found the barrels full of gold and silver and jewels!

The ex-Confederates decided that such a valuable cargo should never be allowed to get out of their hands. The four Austrians and fifteen Mexican peons would be easy to overcome! The following night the caravan was camped at Castle Gap, fifteen miles east of the Horse Head Crossing of the Pecos River. Two Austrians stood guard, walking in opposite circles around the treasure-laden *carretas,* as the Mexicans slept soundly on the ground after the hard day's march.

The six ex-soldiers waited for the signal from their leader. When it came they pounced upon the Austrians and killed them all before the Mexicans were aware of what was going on. Then the Missourians turned their attention to the peons, and one by one they were killed where they slept or were shot down attempting to escape. When the slaughter was over, nineteen dead men lay around the *carretas,* and the treasure belonged to the captors.

After a lengthy discussion the Missourians concluded that it would be unsafe for six men to attempt to move the treasure across the dangerous plains and it would be safer buried in the Gap until more peaceful conditions would permit its recovery.

After taking all the coins each man could carry, a hole was dug in the sandy floor of the canyon, and the fifteen cart loads of gold and silver plate, chests of jewels, and many bags of coin were dumped in. The hole was then partially filled with sand and the dead bodies of the nineteen men thrown in. After the hole had been completely filled and smoothed over, the carts, harness, and canvas were piled on top and set afire, so that the burial site resembled nothing more than a burned-out camp fire. The oxen were turned loose to shift for themselves.

With saddle bags bulging with gold and silver coins, the six Missourians rode away toward San Antonio to spend some of their great fortune and to recruit help in recovering the main body of treasure. Two-days' ride from Castle Gap, one of the ex-soldiers became ill and dropped out for a rest. Thinking this to be a trick designed to recover the treasure for himself, the other five talked over the matter and decided to shoot their companion if he could not travel. Shoot him they did, and he was left beside the trail for dead.

The wounded man, however, recovered in a few days and was able to travel again. Soon he came upon the mutilated bodies of five men, who proved to be his ex-companions. Their empty saddle bags were scattered about, and it was obvious that they had been robbed and killed by bandits. This left the wounded man the sole owner of the great treasure buried in Castle Gap.

For a few days the surviving Missourian struggled on, hiding from Indians, evading outlaws, until one night he happened into the camp of a band of horse thieves. They invited him to stay and he camped down for the night, carefully hiding his bags of coins in the near-by bushes. Before daylight a sheriff's posse surrounded the horse thieves, and the wounded

Missourian, taken for one of them, was thrown in jail with the lot.

Finally securing the services of an attorney, the wounded man was freed, and the lawyer took him to a doctor. The doctor came right out and told the ex-soldier that his wounds were infected and that his chances of living more than a few days were slim indeed. The Missourian was sure that the doctor was wrong, but every day his condition grew worse in spite of everything that was done for him.

Just before the Missourian died he drew a rough map of the treasure site and gave it to the doctor, saying that he had no one to leave the treasure to. Several years later, when the Indian troubles in the area had subsided, the doctor and the attorney took the treasure map and went to Castle Gap. The landmarks shown on the dying Missourian's map could not be located, and no amount of searching in the canyon floor revealed any trace of the fifteen carts, the harness, and other equipment burned there.

Maximilian's treasure, if it still lies under the skeletons of nineteen men, should be worth four or five million dollars to the lucky finder.

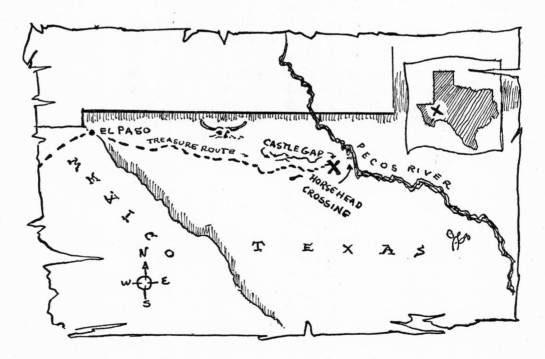

28.

KARL STEINHEIMER'S BURIED MILLIONS

A FEW MILES south of the town of Temple, in central Texas, the Leon and Lampasas rivers unite to form the Little River. As a crow flies, it is perhaps fifty-five miles north and a little east of Austin. Near the junction of these streams a brass spike was once driven into an oak tree to mark the burial place of ten mule loads of gold and silver! The tree may no longer stand, but the fabulous treasure buried by Karl Steinheimer more than one hundred and twenty-five years ago is surely there.

Even as a boy in Germany Karl Steinheimer

longed for a taste of the adventure he read about in books and at the age of eleven, no longer able to stand the dull life of a scholar, he ran away from home. In Hamburg he found exactly what he was looking for—a chance to be a sailor and see the world. He shipped out and for many years he followed the roving, rough life of a seaman, touching at ports all over the world and rubbing elbows with men in all walks of life.

Somewhere among his travels, Steinheimer fell in with a band of smugglers, slave traders, and pirates who had their headquarters on Galveston Island off the coast of Texas. He was aggressive and before long he was struggling with the pirate leader for control of the gang. There was plenty of money for everyone in the profitable slave trade, but Steinheimer wanted power as well as wealth.

When the day finally came for the showdown between the two men, Steinheimer found the odds tremendously against him. He had gambled and lost. There was only one thing to do—capitulate and run.

A few years later Steinheimer found himself in St. Louis, where he met and fell madly in love with a girl whom he asked to marry him. She accepted after some hesitation, and full of good resolutions to settle down, Steinheimer looked around for some kind of a business venture. At the very last moment the girl changed her mind, however, and announced her intention to marry another. The jilted man left St. Louis and

headed south deep into the interior of Mexico. Here he took up prospecting.

Almost from the start Steinheimer was a lucky miner. He acquired holdings and in a few years he was a man of considerable wealth. After some twenty years of fabulously successful mining operations, Steinheimer was visiting in Monterrey where he met an American.

The two men were talking over some drinks when the stranger happened to state that he had recently come from St. Louis. Karl Steinheimer was filled with memories. Perhaps the American might know a certain lady? Yes, indeed, the stranger did know the girl, knew her very well, in fact. Further conversation brought out the fact that his former sweetheart had not married his rival after all! She had never married and she still lived in St. Louis!

With all the wealth that he now possessed, Steinheimer wondered if he might not win the girl after all. At least it was worth trying. After selling out his mining interests, he hired a gang of Mexicans and formed a pack train. Carrying the treasure accumulated over the years, the caravan started north.

It was about the time Texas had declared its independence from Mexico, and the Mexicans, attempting to hold this vast territory, were not friendly to northerners. It was extremely dangerous country to be traveling in and, to make matters worse, Steinheimer was neither Mexican nor Texan. However, the pack train reached Matamoras in safety. There Steinheimer joined

up with a Mexican officer who was about to lead a band of men into Texas in the hope of stirring up an Indian revolt against the Texans.

When the Mexican expedition crossed the Rio Grande into Texas territory and headed north along the old road to San Antonio, Steinheimer and his ten mule loads of treasure brought up the rear. After three days, deciding that a clash between the Mexicans and the Texans was imminent, he left the military party and set out across country with his peons and burros.

A few miles north of Austin he met a party of Mexicans fleeing toward the border, who warned him that the Texans were driving all Mexicans from the country and that many In-
dians were supporting them. Under these very dangerous conditions Steinheimer decided that it would be safest to bury his treasure, leave the country by the shortest possible route, and return to recover his wealth after things had calmed down. He started watching for a spot that would be easy to remember.

A hilly and wooded area near the junction of two streams appeared to be just what he was looking for. Here he made camp and dismissed all the Mexicans in the train except two whom he thought he could trust.

A few feet from a large oak tree Steinheimer and the two Mexicans dug a large pit. Into it they lowered the treasure, filled it in, and carefully tamped down and resodded the earth to avoid discovery. Steinheimer drove a large brass spike into the oak tree to mark the place permanently.

After burying the treasure, Steinheimer and his two companions headed east to get out of Texas as soon as possible. They had not traveled more than a few hours when they were attacked by a band of hostile Indians. The three men barricaded themselves as best they could behind a small knoll. They were hopelessly outnumbered, however, and the two Mexicans were shortly killed. Steinheimer, although wounded, managed to crawl away and hide in the brush. Time after time the Indians almost stepped upon him in searching the area, but they finally left.

Having lost his horse and all of his supplies in the skirmish with the Indians, the wounded man buried the bag of gold he carried with him and, with only a gun and a small quantity of ammunition, set out at night on foot.

Afraid to fire his gun lest the noise attract more Indians, Steinheimer was almost starving when he was overtaken several days later by a party of Texans. His wound was badly infected and he realized that he would probably die before reaching a doctor.

As best he could he drew a rough map of the area where the treasure was buried. Then he wrote a long letter to the girl in St. Louis in which he related the story of the treasure and enclosed the map. If he did not appear in St. Louis in three months, the treasure was to be hers. If, as he feared, he did not appear, she would know that he was dead.

Sealing the envelope, Steinheimer asked the Texans if they would promise to mail the letter in the first town they came to, explaining that the letter was his last farewell to his sister. Seeing that nothing could be done for the ailing man, the Texans agreed.

Several weeks later the letter was delivered to the girl in St. Louis. She remembered Steinheimer well, but was amazed that he would leave her his fortune after being jilted! She showed the letter to relatives, and they decided that conditions were too unsettled in Texas to permit them safely to recover the treasure at that time.

Years later a party of men representing the St. Louis girl went to Texas. They found the junction of the two streams as described, but a long and detailed search failed to reveal the oak tree with the brass spike. The activities of the strangers in the area attracted a lot of attention, and the story of the buried treasure became common knowledge.

Many things could have happened to the old oak tree—but the brass spike, well, it wouldn't just vanish! Perhaps it lies close to the top soil where the tree once stood. Whoever picks it up will be standing close to a fortune of several million dollars!

29.

BARON CASTINE'S BURIED TREASURE

Sieur de Badie, Baron de St. Castine was a man who could stand up to the British soldiers invading the section of Maine that he was carving out as his own little empire, and who could lash out with a defiant tongue at the English governor in Boston. For thirty years he dared to defy both troops and politicians while he was building the fortune treasure hunters still search for on the Pentegoet Peninsula of Maine's rugged coast.

Castine, of noble French background, was educated for the army. Eventually he became a colonel in the élite guards of Louis XIV. Bored with the inactivity of duty in Paris, he asked for an active command in the field. With his regiment he was sent to Quebec where the French control of eastern Canada was being challenged by the British. There he learned to hate the English.

Baron Castine was attracted by the primitive life in North America and he had a way with the Indians. The forests and mountains were full of game, and his shrewd mind soon saw the possibilities of making a fortune in the wilderness country.

When his regiment was ordered back to France, he asked for and secured his release from service. It was rumored at the time that the French officials in Quebec were about to ask for his dismissal anyhow but, true or not, the Baron soon left Canada and journeyed down into the wild and unsettled area of Maine.

On the headland still bearing his name Baron Castine built a trading post and dwelling. Later a fort was added, a long, low irregular structure of heavy logs and stones. Around the whole he erected a stockade. Indians watched warily from the trees but they soon learned that the white man was their friend and that they could trust him.

Twelve guns stolen from the French forces in Canada defended the outpost, and the Baron

119

sent word to the British to stay out of the area. Soon the Indians were bringing in beaver skins by the hundreds and exchanging them for the trinkets and tobacco the trader offered. Year by year Castine's business increased in volume until before long he could boast that he was worth 250,000 crowns in "good dry gold." This was augmented by an inheritance of some 5000 livres a year from his wealthy parents in France.

[In] 1686, no doubt for business reasons, the [Baron marri]ed the daughter of an Indian chief. In a few years the Baron was the most dominant figure in the Penobscot region, and the Indians came to his trading post from far and wide. Sometimes the English came, too, and when they did the Baron met them with angry threats. The King be hanged, screamed the Baron, this was an invasion of his private property and the guns at the fort would speak if they didn't see fit to leave at once.

This was more than the stuffy officials at Boston could tolerate—a direct challenge to British authority. An order was despatched to the Baron to cease obstructing the advance of colonization. The Baron's reply was short and to the point—stay out or suffer the consequences!

Besides being a deuced nuisance, the British concluded that the Baron was a bit mad. At any rate, he had to be taught a lesson. A frigate was sent to dislodge the mad Frenchman and to show him that it didn't pay to insult the British flag. Seeing that he was outnumbered, the Baron fled to the woods and watched helplessly as the English soldiers destroyed the guns and ammunition he had been forced to abandon.

After raiding his post of furniture and provisions, the Englishmen sailed away. Word soon arrived from the Governor in Boston that all would be forgiven and his property returned if the Baron would ally himself with the British cause and promise to behave himself. The Baron's spirit was hardly dented, however, and he replied that he had no such intentions. Instead, he would call upon his Indian friends for reprisals.

During the next fifteen years the mad Baron carried on his one-man war with the British, strongly supported by his Indian friends who had seen enough of British trickery. In the meantime he continued to prosper and to add to his holdings. Then business demanded his presence in France. It was decided that his daughter's husband would accompany him.

Before sailing, Baron Castine told his daughter where his wealth was buried and briefed her in the care of the post. In the event of an attack by the British she was to flee to the woods until the invaders departed. He would be gone a long time.

The Baron had no more than arrived in France when Major Church sailed up Penobscot Bay with a regiment of redcoats. Taking her small child and a bag of coins, Castine's daughter followed instructions and fled into the forest. Before she could reach the friendly Indians, however, the British overtook her. Near the Narrows of the Bagaduce River she managed to cache the coins.

The fate of Castine's daughter was never determined, but presumably the British held her awaiting the Baron's return. The Baron, however, never arrived. While in France he became ill and died.

In November 1849, an old sea captain, Stephen Grindle, and his son Samuel were dragging logs along the banks of the Bagaduce about six miles from the site of the old Castine trading post. The two were walking along a path through the shrubbery when the boy noticed a coin lying in the rut made by one of the logs. He picked it up and examined it.

The coin was worn bright from the log's being dragged over it and was easily identified as French and more than two hundred years old. They poked around in the dirt for more coins and before darkness forced them to quit they found twenty more. The first big snow of the winter fell that evening, and the ground was covered until the thaws of the following April, when the search was resumed.

Close to the Narrows a coin was found attached to a stone with moss. Near by was a small ledge of rocks, and poking into this ledge the old captain found the coins cached by Baron Castine's daughter in her unsuccessful flight from the British.

Later in the same month a second search of the area was made and a few more old coins were recovered. About 2000 coins were picked up, consisting of English, French, Peruvian, Dutch, and Spanish pieces. Dates indicated strongly that this was part of the Castine hoard and they have been so labeled by the Maine Historical Society in Portland where part of the find is on permanent exhibit.

A concentrated search was made later for the main treasure buried by the mad Baron in a tin box near the old fort on Pentegoet Peninsula, but it has never been found. As stubbornly as the old Baron defied the English, his treasure has defied all who have sought it.

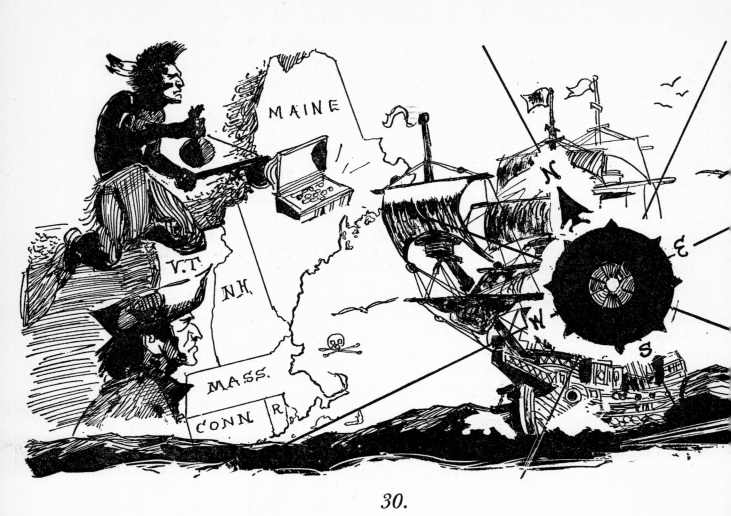

30.

THE BURIED TREASURES OF NEW ENGLAND

PIRATES, BANDITS, OUTLAWS, SOLDIERS, SPANISH miners, and robbers have all added to the rich treasure lore of the New England states. People of Colonial times were great story tellers and they handed down many tales that, enlarged with each telling, have resulted in the accumulation of a great many legendary treasure stories. Who can tell where legend stops and fact begins?

The New England states comprise Maine, Vermont, New Hampshire, Rhode Island, Connecticut, and Massachusetts, all of which, except Vermont, have a sea coast. Almost every inch of this coastline was touched upon by the early pirates. Casco Bay in Maine, the Isle of Shoals off New Hampshire, and Block Island off Rhode Island were all pirate hideouts for such

notorious characters as John Quelch, Dixie Bull, William Kidd, Captain Bellamy, William Teach, and a host of others. Each left a memento of his stay in buried treasure.

Up in Vermont there is a treasure story of an unusual nature. At three o'clock on the cloudy afternoon of October 18, 1864, the streets of St. Albans were almost empty except for a number of men who loitered about in the vicinity of the three banks located near the green. No one thought anything of their presence, but at the moment the town clock struck three, they quietly formed into three separate groups and converged upon the three unsuspecting banks. One man in each group carried a leather satchel slung over his shoulder.

Inside the banks the strangers pulled out their

revolvers and demanded the cash. In the First National Bank the raiders seized $57,000. The St. Albans Bank contributed $73,522, but the bandits overlooked another $50,000 in signed, but uncut notes. In the Franklin County Bank $70,000 was scooped up and thrown into a leather pouch.

Outside on Main Street, which was a mire of mud from recent rains, other members of the gang had rounded up stray citizens and were holding them at gun point while their companions completed their appointed jobs. Down the street a shot sounded, then another. St. Albans was rousing from its temporary paralysis at last. Revolvers in hand, the robbers emerged from the banks and made a dash for the horses brought up by their companions. The shooting grew in intensity as puzzled citizens fired into the air from near-by windows, not certain what was taking place or why they were firing.

A young photographer dashed out of his shop and, bumping into one of the outlaws, said, "What's the celebration, mister?" "I'll let you know," the bandit shouted back. He fired and missed.

Organized at last and unharmed by all the wild shooting, the raiders rode off, leaving a storm of mud thrown up by their horses and shooting a wild farewell at anything in sight.

Vermont had been raided by the Confederacy! Rail traffic was halted, and steamers on Lake Champlain were moved out into the water. Troops were rushed to the frontier town and a posse immediately set out in pursuit. The First National Bank offered a reward of $10,000 for the return of its money.

It was less than fifteen miles to the Canadian border and the raiders made good their escape, but fourteen of the twenty-two Confederate soldiers were later picked up in Canada, carrying but $86,000 of the $200,522 seized from the three banks. They claimed that the remainder of the treasure, $114,522, was buried before they crossed the border. It has never been found.

The little town of Bristol is about fifty-five miles due south of St. Albans. Just outside the village limits is a weird wall of fantastically tumbled boulders broken by cracks, crevices, and deep caverns and known to the natives as "Hell's Half Acre." This is the scene of the famous Bristol Money Diggings.

In about 1800 a strange old man appeared in Bristol and, after spending many days poking in and out of the Hell's Half Acre area, he told a strange treasure story. He said that his name was De Grau, that he was a Spaniard, and that as a boy he was a member of an expedition to

Susannah. Since the *San José,* carrying a cargo valued at almost half a million dollars and forty chests of silver and one chest of gold, was in no immediate danger, it was agreed that it follow the American to New London, Connecticut.

Entering New London Harbor, the American

Canada with a fabulous amount of treasure. On the way they were attacked by Indians. The Spaniards hurriedly buried the treasure in the rocks around Bristol and escaped. De Grau was an old man before he was able to get back to Bristol and he was uncertain just where the treasure was hidden.

Several Bristol citizens helped make a systematic search but they eventually concluded that the earthquake of 1755 had changed the landscape and probably buried the treasure even deeper. De Grau finally died in Bristol but the digging of later treasure hunters has literally covered the area with empty holes.

There is some reason to believe that the old man's story may not be as fantastic as it sounds when all the pieces are put together. In 1752 the Spanish ship *San José* sprang a leak off the coast of Cuba, and her distress signal was answered by the captain of the American ship,

pilot grounded the *San José,* and the treasure was transferred to the *Susannah* and taken on into the port. Here it was seized by the governor and placed in a warehouse until its disposition could be determined. While the angry Spaniards cooled their heels, the authorities wrangled over the treasure. When eventually the Spaniards were told that the treasure would be released to them, they chartered the *Nebuchadnezzar* to carry the cargo to Spain.

Meanwhile some of the Spaniards had left New London, and when the remainder of the party went to the warehouse to claim their cargo they found only 305 pieces of silver out of the original 83,600 pieces—and the 5100 pieces of gold had shrunk to 480 pieces! Who had stolen the treasure? No one knows, of course, but the finger of suspicion points to the missing Spaniards—and one of them may have, indeed, been De Grau!

Somewhere between Smith's Pond and Portsmouth, New Hampshire, the Tory Governor, John Wentworth, buried his treasure when he and his wife fled toward Canada at the start of the Revolution. The seven chests of silverware and money proved too great a burden for their twenty servants and their horses, and it was cached along the route, never to be recovered.

For more than one hundred and fifty years treasure hunters have searched the hills around Dalton, Massachusetts. After General Burgoyne was defeated at Saratoga, New York, his hired Hessian soldiers fled in the general direction of Boston, carrying with them the money and jewels they had accumulated in months of pillage. As the angry colonial farmers closed in on them, they stuffed their treasure in the muzzles of howitzers which they buried somewhere in the vicinity of Dalton.

Off the coast of New Hampshire the Isle of Shoals is famed as the burial place of treasure belonging to no fewer than three pirate leaders —Captain William Kidd, John Quelch, and Blackbeard. Some of this treasure was recovered in 1704 by Massachusetts authorities who were searching the islands for other pirates, and part of Blackbeard's treasure was found many years later.

Every summer finds men digging in the sands along the shores of Block Island nine miles south of the Rhode Island mainland. Both Captain Kidd and Joe Bradish are said to have buried treasure on the island before being taken to England and hanged. Bradish gave a companion a map showing the burial place of his treasure, but the latter never returned from England where he went to testify for Bradish during his trial.

Boston Harbor is dotted with islands and rocks, each with its own treasure story. Deer Island was the scene of the discovery of old coins in 1906, and many searches have been made since then for the treasure of the schooner *Juliet* wrecked offshore in 1886. Less than a mile from Deer Island is Lovell's Island, scene of a score of shipwrecks, the most spectacular of which was that of the French warship *Magnifique* which is claimed to have carried a considerable fortune in her strong box. Part of the treasure is believed to have been recovered. Castle and Snake islands have both been the scene of treasure hunts, and $5000 was found hidden in a cave on Hog Island in 1846, where Captain Kidd is said to have buried a chest of gold. Apple Island and Conant's Island have been searched thoroughly for pirate treasure, and Calf Island concealed for many years a clue that led to the uncovering of a treasure chest on Cape Cod by Edward Rowe Snow.

In the islands dotting Casco Bay, Maine, treasure stories are as thick as trees, and innumerable searches have been made for the treasure supposedly buried there by the pirates Lowe, Kidd, Blackbeard, and Dixie Bull. Remains of the earthwork fort of Captain Bellamy are still visible at Machias, Maine, and the pirate is said to have buried an enormous treasure along the banks of the Machias River.

Actually, there is hardly any section of New England that does not have a buried treasure story and these are but a few. Treasure is where you find it—and you find it where it was hidden, unless someone beats you to it!

31

PLANTATION TREASURES OF LOUISIANA

THE YANKEES ARE COMING!" was a familiar cry throughout the South during the Civil War. It was the signal for the hiding of family valuables and the burying of treasure!

Long before the United States acquired Louisiana, there existed a wealthy French aristocracy of planters, who owned immense grants of land along the Mississippi River and the many bayous. They prospered and lived in the grand manner of French noblemen with thousands of acres tilled by slave workers. Their furniture and china, the very finest, was imported from Europe, and many a plantation could boast of service of solid gold.

Even in this elegant and expensive manner of living, the grand old planters could spend but a small portion of their fortune and so handed it down from generation to generation. Where did they keep it? In their magnificent plantation mansions, of course. When the Yankees arrived the only thing they could do was bury it. Many never returned, or returning, were unable to locate the treasure hidden in such hurry. Hardly a plantation stands in Louisiana without its story of buried treasure. Here are but a few of them.

Grand Coteau is a little town in the heart of the Evangeline country about ten miles southeast of Opelousas. Here the wealthy Frenchman, Fusilier de la Claire, built his plantation home, which had twice been passed from father to son. One night, during the Civil War, a dinner party was in full progress at the Claire plantation in honor of the soldiers who were home on leave. Suddenly word arrived that the Yankees were approaching.

The young master of the house and a trusted slave gathered the great wealth kept in the house and hurriedly buried it in the garden. When they returned to the house, the other servants were disguising the soldiers as runaway slaves in the hope that they could slip through the Union lines to safety.

The Confederate soldiers made good their escape, and the Union troops entered the house to find a small group of slaves huddled in the candlelight. Hearing that they had been outwitted, the Union commander ordered the house fired, and with its contents, it was burned to the ground. After the war the remaining members of the Claire family tried to recover the treasure but it was never found.

Chrétien Point was another magnificent plantation home located in the Bayou Teche country west of New Orleans. The vast holdings of the Chrétien family dated back to Spanish days, and Jean and Pierre Lafitte had often visited Chrétien Point. Some claim the dashing corsairs even buried part of their treasure here.

Hippolyte Chrétien II was one of those men, not rare in his day, who believed that money was safer buried in the ground. He buried his beneath the trees in the garden, and only he and an old Negro named Pajo knew its exact location. When Felicité, his wife, complained that she wouldn't be able to find the treasure if he died, Hippolyte said he wasn't figuring on dying for awhile. It wasn't long, however, before Hippolyte was dead of fever.

Just as she had predicted, Felicité failed to find the money, and old Pajo would talk only vaguely. Finally she decided that Hippolyte had moved the treasure to another site. Two more generations searched the grounds many times before the fine old mansion was lost to moneylenders. Treasure hunters still dig for the heavy chests buried by Felicité's husband.

Up the river from New Orleans, on a bayou called False River, Marquis Vincent de Ternant built a costly and elegant mansion out of his vast sugar profits. Outside it was all French Louisianan; inside it was direct from Paris— carved mahogany furniture, inlaid tables, hand-painted china, gold-framed mirrors, and glittering chandeliers.

The third master of the mansion on False River was Colonel Charles Parlange of the French army, and his wife, Virginie, was a French girl of Louisiana birth. The estate became known, and is to this day, as Parlange.

The Civil War came and Virginie—her husband had died many years before—decided to keep her estate intact from the Yankees. The only way to do this, she reasoned, was to hide everything of value. Her fine silverware was hidden in the walls, the best furniture was stored in the attic, and three large chests of gold, amounting to more than $300,000, were buried in three separate places under the huge liveoaks in the gardens.

Virginie met the Union soldiers at the door and invited them in. She served them fine wine and food. When the soldiers left Parlange, nothing was taken and the only damage done was the trampling of the rose bushes in the gardens where the Yankees had stabled their horses.

When the war was over, the hidden valuables were gradually brought from hiding. The silver was all there and the furniture was as good as new, but only one of the three treasure chests could be found although much digging and hunting was done in an effort to recover them.

Valcour Aime, once known as "the little Versailles of Louisiana," stands in utter ruins today, its gardens a tangled mass of vines and trees, its proud old walls no more than a pile of rubble. Here Valcour Aime, reputed to be the richest man in the South, lived the life of a feudal lord. His lavish receptions and other entertainments are remembered in St. James Parish to this day.

On one occasion Valcour Aime won a $10,000 bet from an epicure by serving a perfect dinner, all of which—fish, game, fruits, nuts, coffee, cigars, and wine—was supplied from the immediate plantation. He operated a steamboat between his plantation and New Orleans for his own convenience and that of his guests and named it the *Gabriel Aime* in honor of his only son.

Five beautiful daughters were born to Josephine and Valcour Aime, all of whom married into wealthy plantation families, but the pride and joy of the Frenchman's life was Gabriel. When Gabriel finally returned from Paris and prepared to settle down at Valcour Aime, there was great joy in the household. A few days later Gabriel was dead of fever. His father, broken-hearted, never recovered from his grief, and the plantation was never the same again.

In a few years Josephine, too, was gone, and one by one old Valcour buried his five daughters. He had only his fortune left, and this was worthless to a man who wanted to die. When the Civil War came, Valcour Aime and an old

colored man were the only people living on the plantation where once thirty slaves were required to care for the gardens alone. When word was brought to the aging man that the Yankees were about to arrive, he and the old slave loaded the family treasure into a cart and hauled it to a spot in the neglected gardens. Here it was buried, and it has never been recovered.

The history of the old plantation house of d'Estrehan is long and interesting and has its share of tragedy. It started with the Frenchmen, Pierre and Jean Trepagnier who rose as mighty rulers under the Spanish regime in Louisiana and counted themselves among the first families in the colony. Both were beaten to death by an angry mob of Negroes, an act that brought about a furious revenge.

The remaining Trepagniers left for France, and the house drifted into other hands, eventually becoming the property of Jean Noel d'Estrehan, the father of fourteen children and a man who could match the wealth of the richest man in Louisiana.

At the height of his career the pirate Jean Lafitte and his brother Pierre frequently visited

tation home near here and amassed a fortune in sugar growing. Early in the nineteenth century the slaves killed Thibodeaux and made off with his hoard of gold. A short distance from the house they buried the treasure when they found it too heavy to carry. A posse caught up with the fleeing slaves and executed its own brand of justice. The treasure was never found.

Treasure has been found in many places in Louisiana—German coins at Bayou Chicot near Opelousas, English silver at Ruston, Spanish doubloons at Baton Rouge and New Orleans—and the search for more goes on constantly. A treasure hunt at Pecan Island reached such enthusiastic proportions that giant oak trees were uprooted and pits were left in the ground that are still visible today. A plantation house on the

the house, and many people believe that the brothers buried part of their treasure there. Today the house still stands along the bank of the Mississippi and is used as a clubhouse for employees of the Pan American Oil Company.

Beaux Bridge is a quiet little town in St. Martin Parish. Narcisse Thibodeaux built his plan-

river road near Ste. Rose has been totally razed by treasure hunters, its floor torn up tile by tile.

A huge billboard on Highway U.S. 90 three and one-half miles east of the bridge across the Sabine River, which separates Louisiana and Texas, announces for all who are concerned: "Lafitte Buried His Treasure Here Near 40 Gum Trees!" Yes, Louisiana is a treasure state!

32.

THE BURIED TREASURE OF PADRE ISLAND

PADRE ISLAND is one of a long chain of sandy offshore islands extending from Louisiana to Mexico. Sometimes Padre is one island, at other times it is two or more islands, for the winds, the tides, and the crashing waves make a plaything of it, closing one old bisecting channel, opening new ones. You never know whether Padre will be there tomorrow.

Corpus Christi Pass separates Padre from Mustang Island to the north, but the pass is frequently closed after a hard storm and the two islands are locally referred to as one. From the northern tip of Mustang to the southern tip of Padre is a distance of one hundred and thirty miles, but at no point is the island more than three or four miles wide.

Resembling a huge crescent, Padre guards with its long slender form the main coastline of Texas, from which it is separated by Laguna Madre. Padre is, in fact, nothing but an enormous sandbar, but every foot of its sandy soil is steeped in treasure lore. It is doubtful if any similar area in the world has been searched over for treasure as consistently as Padre. It is the treasure hunter's paradise!

First, there was the Spanish treasure fleet, bulging with gold and silver, that was wrecked on the shores of Padre in 1553. Caught in the whiplash of a furious storm, the vessels were lashed across the Gulf and hurled like paper boats against Padre's glistening shores. Three hundred or so crewmen and passengers escaped death by the sea only to be cut down later by Indian arrows or to die in the scorching heat along the route to Mexico.

As late as 1853 Lafitte's old embankments and fortifications were still visible on Padre, and along the beach were many posts with iron rings, which were used for tying up the small boats that plied between the shore and the larger craft riding at anchor in the open water.

At least two of Lafitte's ships, both carrying treasure, are said to have been wrecked off Padre. Lafitte himself is said to have buried a large fortune under a millstone on whose surface were inscribed the words: "Dig Deeper."

The beaches of Padre have long been a favorite place for picnics, and part of the fun is poking in the sand with iron rods in the hope that a treasure chest will be discovered. During one of these picnic jaunts many years ago, two children reported to their parents that they had found a

It was months before the loss of the ships was known in Spain, and it was not until April 1554 that the salvage ships arrived and dropped anchor off Padre. With grappling hooks and a kind of a crude diving bell, native divers from Yucatan finally succeeded in recovering part of the treasure, but most of it still rests in the sands of the island or in the water offshore.

With Jean Lafitte's pirate treasure reportedly buried in a hundred different places from Mobile Bay to Port Isabel, it is inevitable that Padre would claim a share of it. While maintaining his headquarters at Galveston, the striking figure of the French privateer was often seen at Corpus Christi, and his vessels used the protected waters of Laguna Madre as a haven during the hurricane season.

large round stone half buried in the sand dunes. They had played around the rock all day, using it as a table. One of the men in the party recalled the story of Lafitte's treasure under the millstone. On the following day he returned to the island with a search party and they combed the area. During the night, however, the wind had covered the children's tracks and not a trace of the stone could be found. Every dune looked exactly like thousands of other dunes, and if Lafitte's chest was under that stone, it is probably still there.

When the remnants of Lafitte's forces were driven from Galveston, many of them drifted down to Padre and took up residence on the sandy island. These bands of men used false lights and fake signals to lure unsuspecting ships to their doom on the bars and shell banks. A favorite trick was to tie a lighted lantern to the neck of a hobbled burro. The bobbing light resembled a schooner at anchor in the gentle waters of an inlet. The result was frequently a wrecked ship and easily salvaged loot.

After 1840 most of Lafitte's followers on Padre began to be replaced by men of more respectable habits. Among these was John V. Singer whose name is still connected with one of the many treasure hoards of the island.

Singer, with his wife and several sons, was cast up on Padre in 1847 when his three-masted schooner, the *Alice Sadell,* was blown too far inshore and broke to pieces on the surf at the southern end of the island. Somehow he and all his family managed to get ashore although the entire crew of the ship was lost.

A man of great physical reserve, Singer decided to remain on Padre and salvage the treasure along the island's shores. His wife, Johanna, agreed. Together they built a tent from the salvaged sails of the wrecked schooner and secured enough stores to live on. Finally they collected enough timbers from wrecked vessels to build a small house. Here they lived for many years, combing the beaches for wreckage and poking into the sand for treasure.

It wasn't many years before Singer was able to buy a portion of the island from interests representing the original grantee, Padre Nicolas Balli, after whom the island was named. Moving his family further southward, Singer and his sons built a fine residence from salvaged materials. A blacksmith shop and corrals followed.

Year after year Singer's holdings on the island increased—and so did the size of his family, six children being born on the island. They stocked cattle and before many years the very successful Singer family was branding as many as fifteen hundred head a year. More land was purchased; more cattle stocked; more wrecks salvaged. The children often jingled old Spanish coins in their pockets, the fruitful results of tramps along the beach, they said.

When the Civil War started, the Singers were loud in their praises of the Confederate cause. They were driven from the island and, according to a story later told by the oldest son, they had left in such a hurry that they could not take their treasure with them. It was buried in stone jars in four feet of sand near the ranch house.

Before the Singers could return to Padre, Federal forces occupied the island and set up headquarters at the Singer ranch. The Singer cattle were slaughtered to feed the troops, and when they eventually left, nothing remained of the ranch but a ruined house, a few outbuildings, and the stumps of the posts where the corrals once stood.

Before they could rebuild their house, Johanna Singer died, and her husband took up his life at sea once more. The children were scattered, some of the boys serving on the Union side and others joining the Confederates. Alexander, the eldest, returned to Padre and made a

search for the family treasure. He found about $2000 but the main portion of the treasure has never been located.

About 1868 old John Singer himself came back to Padre and searched for his treasure. By this time, however, all remains of the buildings were obliterated by the shifting sands and he could locate none of his markers.

Many articles are still picked up on Padre after a heavy storm has all but blown the island out of the water, including peculiarly shaped stones which natives are sure were once used to mark the sites of buried treasure. Mexicans, they explain, used to carry on a thriving smuggling business the length of the island. Gold and silver in stout bags were smuggled out of Mexico into the United States and traded for articles that were more valuable in Mexico. When the smugglers were trailed by the law or by robbers, they had to bury their treasure in a hurry. To mark its burial site they used the marked stones, which were, of course, covered almost immediately by the winds.

Hurricanes are one of the best agents in the recovery of treasure. In 1933 a storm cut a new channel across Padre at the point where Union soldiers had camped many years before. Exposed by the winds and the waves were a great variety of articles including bullets, coins, buttons, bottles, watches, leather boots and belts, and endless articles common to military life.

The probability of recovering treasure on Padre Island is good. Doubloons, pieces of eight, rotting chests, jewelry, and many items connected with buried treasure are found from time to time. New storms will uncover new finds.

33.

THE BURIED TREASURES OF FLORIDA

CLOSE TO TROPICAL SEAS, skirted by coral reefs, washed by the Gulf Stream, and swept by the trade winds, Florida's lonely coasts, so lately pirate-haunted, are ideal sites for buried treasure and have not lacked attention from treasure hunters.

Florida is a great golden horseshoe from which pirates operated almost at will, cutting down rich treasure-laden galleons and taking cover in the recesses of her thousands of coves, bays, and rivers to divide the loot. Nature, too, contributed to the treasure lore of the Florida coast by flinging scores of hurricane-tossed ships to their doom on her sands and shoals. Yes, Florida is a treasure hunter's paradise!

Of the pirates who frequented the Florida waters in vast numbers, Gasparilla is the best remembered for his deeds and for his fabulous treasure.

Born in Spain José Gaspár, son of a wealthy and respected family, he was in trouble and the black sheep of the family from the time he entered the Spanish navy at an early age until his dramatic death in 1821. Standing in high favor at the Spanish court because of his family background, Gaspár was one day entrusted with the royal jewels. Instead of delivering the jewels as instructed, he stole a ship, recruited some of the shipmates he had fascinated with stories of the Spanish Main, and sailed off to become a pirate.

Adopting the name "Gasparilla," which means "Little Gaspár," the young pirate selected Charlotte Harbor on the west coast of Florida as his base of operations and erected a palace and fort on the island now known as Gasparilla. Being a well-educated man and one of polished manners, the pirate lost no time in creating a kingdom and declaring himself king of the pirates.

From his Charlotte Harbor lair Gasparilla roamed the Gulf and the Spanish Main in search of prizes. According to his own records, he captured thirty-six ships, carrying an enormous amount of treasure, in the eleven years between 1784 and 1795. His male prisoners were offered their choice of joining the pirate band or walking the plank.

One day he overpowered a Spanish vessel carrying a princess and eleven beautiful Mexican girls back to Spain. Aboard their ship were their dowry chests filled with gold. Gasparilla took the girls to Captiva Island, just south of Charlotte Harbor, and turned them over to his men for wives. When the princess spurned the offer to become his queen, he had her beheaded.

For several years Gasparilla had everything his own way and amassed a fortune estimated at $30,000,000, but this could not go on indefinitely. One day in 1821 his ship was weighing anchor and preparing to sail away on another pirate cruise when a strange ship was seen entering Charlotte Harbor. It appeared to be a British merchant ship, and Gasparilla decided to add it to his long list of victims. Before he could swing his ship into action, however, the United States flag fluttered up to the masthead of the approaching ship and a broadside roared from her hidden guns. There was no chance to escape as his ship was terribly damaged and the odds were too great to fight back. Gasparilla, determined not to be taken alive, wrapped himself in heavy chains and, shouting words of defiance, jumped overboard!

The Gasparilla millions are reportedly buried somewhere on Gasparilla Island or on the mainland around Charlotte Harbor. Although the pirate kept an accurate diary of his activities for many years he never, of course, recorded the hiding place of his treasure. The vessel sunk by the American gunboat off Gasparilla Island is supposed to have carried down $1,000,000, and many attempts have been made to recover it.

All of the Florida Keys extending from Miami to Key West have been the scenes of intensive

treasure hunts, and many hoards have been found on the islands or in the waters offshore. An unidentified sunken ship lies off Soldier Key with $2,000,000 in her rusting hulk, and Long Key was the scene of the wreckage in 1715 of fourteen Spanish treasure galleons, carrying an estimated $65,000,000, of which some has been recovered.

The Spanish galleon *Santa Rosa* with the ransom gold paid Cortéz by Montezuma and valued at $30,000,000, lies embedded in the coral off Key West. Grassy Key, where treasure has already been found, is searched for treasure buried in the ground. Money Key was so named because of the treasure found there, and more is sought. Key Largo is a region rich in treasure lore, and pirate treasure is said to be buried on the island.

Panther Key, Elliott's Key, Old Matecumbe, Duck Key, Upper Matecumbe, and Captain's Key, among others, are all known to have yielded treasure at one time or another, but you don't have to be selective in searching for treasure among the Florida Keys—select the Key that appeals to you. There is treasure there!

But the treasures of Florida are not all of pirate origin. The Spanish gunboat supposedly sunk in the mouth of the Suwannee River with $5,000,000 aboard has been the object of many searchers. The vessel was carrying minted coins transferred from a United States vessel at Pensacola. Crossing the Gulf the ship encountered a sudden storm and was blown to shore, striking a bar and sinking at the mouth of the Suwannee.

History tells us that the Spanish grandee, Ponce de León, came to Florida looking for the fabled Fountain of Youth. Actually, the story was first written many years after Ponce de León's death by a youth named Fontenada, who was merely repeating a Caribbean legend about a river in which a man could regain his health and youth. Ponce de León came to Florida, reportedly with a great quantity of gold and silver, to establish his claim to a patent of land granted by the Holy Roman Emperor, Charles V. Finding the Indians hostile, he buried the greater part of his wealth near De León Springs where a treasure chest was sup-

posedly recovered and then lost again in 1888.

Many bandits and outlaws have made the Everglades their hiding place from the law. The last of these organized gangs were the Ashleys who terrorized Florida banks from 1915 to 1926 and made their headquarters near the village of Canal Point at the southern tip of Lake Okeechobee. They reportedly buried $110,000 at a secret lair someplace in the Everglades and it has never been located.

Another treasure supposedly secreted in the swamplands of the Everglades is $500,000 in Confederate gold bullion. About half a ton of gold was being transported by a Captain Riley and some soldiers to Havana, Cuba. Fearing that Union soldiers were about to overtake them, they buried the gold deep in the Everglades. The last camping place of the Confederate soldiers convoying the gold was reportedly found several years ago, but the treasure is still resting in the heart of the great Everglades wastelands.

Wrecked treasure ships literally encircle the coast of Florida, and only a few can be mentioned here. Under the waters of Choctawhatchee Bay are the wrecks of a dozen pirate ships. Farther down the coast, near Apalachicola, is a place on the coast highway where a sign reads "Money Bayou." Here, it is said, the pirate Copeland buried three kegs of treasure. Near St. Marks the pirate Lewis Leland made his headquarters and is said to have buried a great quantity of treasure.

On Sanibel Island the huge Negro pirate, Black Caesar, spent his last years and supposedly buried his wealth. The fabulously rich Spanish galleon, *Santa Margarita*, with millions in her hold is wrecked off Palm Beach. Treasure has been found at New River Sound but the greater part is said still to be covered in tons of sand. A treasure ship was driven ashore by a hurricane and sunk about nine miles north of Ft. Lauderdale. Thirteen surviving seamen recovered part of the treasure and carried it about four miles north where it became too heavy and they buried it.

Yes, if it is treasure you are looking for, Florida is the place! You will at least have fun!

34.

THE GREATEST TREASURE OF THEM ALL

SOMEWHERE IN NORTHWESTERN NEW MEXICO is a buried treasure hoard of $20,000,000 in Mexican gold ingots. It has been buried in an isolated spot for about twenty years, and at least one man knows exactly where that spot is!

Rumors of the gold hoard have been current among Federal officials for several years. Treasury Department officials are interested in finding the fabulous hoard because it is in direct violation of the Gold Reserve Act of 1934 which prohibits the holding of gold except for specified purposes.

According to the best information available at this time, the gold was accumulated by a Mexican citizen and brought to the United States about 1933 because of uncertain conditions in Mexico. Twenty million dollars in gold isn't accumulated very easily, and both Mexican and United States officials are wondering just how this man accomplished the feat!

Mexico is full of isolated places ideal for hiding such a vast quantity of treasure. Why, then, was it brought to the United States? One doesn't throw $20,000,000 worth of gold on a mule and head for the mountains for no good reason! And how was it brought here and transported to a remote spot in New Mexico?

Shortly after the gold was brought into the United States a law became effective making it necessary for anyone holding gold or gold notes to turn them over to the United States Treasury for which they were reimbursed with paper money. Penalties were provided to punish violators of this law.

For some reason known only to himself, the owner of the $20,000,000 did not comply with the law. About two years ago a man representing the owner of the gold approached United States officials and attempted to arrange a sale to the United States Mint without suffering any penalties. The offer was rejected, and Secret Service agents started an exhaustive investigation of the story.

Later several prominent Southern California men were approached to act as intermediaries in an attempt to sell the gold to the mint. One of these men reputedly acts with power of attorney from the owner. The Federal officials, however, take the position that the gold hoard must first be seized by the Government and the owner must bring suit to prove his legal ownership. If this man knows anything about the slow, cumbersome processes of Federal law in the United States, he probably figures that he would be dead before a decision could be reached!

In September 1952 the matter of the hoarded gold came up before the Federal Grand Jury in Los Angeles. Before that body appeared an escrow officer of the First National Bank of Ontario (California) with records showing that an escrow had been set up as a means of selling the gold to the United States. The only information gathered other than the facts given up to then was that the gold was hidden in northwestern New Mexico!

It seems to be definitely established that this fabulous hoard actually exists, and you can be certain that many a treasure hunter has cast his eyes over a map of New Mexico wondering what on earth he would do with almost twenty tons of gold ingots even if he did find them!

Strangely enough, the hoard is practically worthless as long as the original owner still lives at the time it is found and is not afraid to step up and establish his ownership. In this event the gold would be either turned over to him— after penalties were exacted, of course—or confiscated by the Federal government. If the legal owner was not found, the Government might share part of it with the finder. It is hard to say in this case.

Here is a very good example of the manner in

which many lost treasures become "lost." Suppose the owner of this great treasure hoard gives up his attempts to sell the gold to the United States. What is he going to do with it? Although it was apparently smuggled into the United States, it is quite unlikely that it can be smuggled out because you can be sure that customsmen are watching closely for that.

find a million spots in which twenty tons of gold could be dropped and covered up without effacing the landscape the slightest bit!

If this, the greatest of all treasures to be buried in our country in modern times, is lost, then it may well be found someday by a man of science for New Mexico is the camping ground of archaeologists and anthropologists who poke

Not being able to move the treasure, the owner keeps his secret to himself and finally goes to his grave with it. Years pass and the story is all but forgotten, popping up now and then to intrigue treasure hunters. With every retelling of the mystery the facts are dimmed and the hoard grows in value from twenty to fifty, to a hundred million dollars!

New Mexico is a huge country—even the northwestern quarter of it—with rugged mountains, mesas, buttes, cliffs, and canyons traversing it in all directions. It would not be hard to

constantly into every crevice and cranny in search of artifacts of the past.

Four hundred and fifteen years ago a group of Spaniards known as the conquistadores came to New Mexico looking for the fabulous treasures of the famed Seven Cities of Cibola. Their goal was northwestern New Mexico, and there they found the seven cities of the Zunis as Estevanico, the Black Moor, said they would— but there was no treasure! Today the treasure is there—twenty tons of it! Indeed, you may follow in the footsteps of the Spanish conquistadors!

35.

TREASURE CODE AND SIGNS

M OST PEOPLE who bury treasure do not trust their memory to lead them back to the spot when they are ready to recover their wealth. Usually a map or rough chart is prepared showing the outstanding landmarks of the vicinity such as trees, streams, boulders, hills, and valleys. But charts can become lost, and after many years it is often difficult to follow the best plotted set of directions.

The path leading to buried treasure and even to the burial spot itself is often marked with symbols carved on trees or chiseled on rocks. The early Spaniards of the Southwest buried a great deal of treasure and they were particularly likely to leave permanent symbols, many of which have been discovered in Arizona, New Mexico and Texas. Some have actually led to the finding of buried treasure. The more common buried treasure signs are shown here together with their meaning.

Cross on its side. The long part of the horizontal bar points in the direction of the treasure or to the next marker.

Upright cross. Treasure is buried below. The cross usually indicates Church treasure, though not always for the early Spaniards were in the habit of marking their trails with a series of crosses.

Horizontal arrow. Points toward treasure or next marker. In the Southwest often used to indicate the way to water.

Arrow pointed upward. Follow to other markers farther on.

Arrow pointing downward. Treasure underneath. Length of shaft may sometimes indicate the depth of treasure.

Crossed arrows. Treasure has been divided into as many parts as there are arrows and buried in the directions indicated.

Flying arrow. Wrong direction. Retrace steps to last marker and proceed again.

Knife. Point indicates direction of buried treasure. More common throughout the Southwest than in other sections of the country.

Dirk. Point indicates direction of buried treasure. Usually indicates pirate treasure.

Turtle. The head indicates way to treasure. Sometimes used as a warning or danger sign.

Snake heading up a tree. Treasure lies farther on in the direction indicated by the opposite side of the tree.

Snake heading down a tree. Treasure is buried below. The length of the snake's tail and the distance from the tip of the tail to the ground may indicate the depth of the treasure.

Coiled snake. Treasure is buried directly underneath. If chiseled on a rock, the treasure is under the rock.

Horizontal mule shoe. Treasure is ahead. Keep going in the direction indicated by the arc of the shoe.

Mule shoe with toe pointing down. Treasure is underneath. Toe pointing up indicates treasure is farther on.

Wigwams. Indians in the vicinity, their numbers indicated by the number of wigwams.

Wigwam with smoke. Treasure is buried in the vicinity of Indian village.

Sun. Indicates treasure buried in the immediate vicinity.

Gourd. Points to water or indicates that treasure is buried near a spring.

Peace pipe. Treasure is buried near camp or in the country of friendly Indians.

Forest. Treasure is buried in forest or you must travel through forest to arrive at burial place.

Sombrero. The number of people in the party burying the treasure are indicated by the number of sombreros. Sometimes the sombreros indicate the number of people killed in burying the treasure or in transporting it to the burial site.

Moose. The long line of the body points the way to the treasure cache. This sign was frequently used by Indians, seldom by the Spaniards.

Rectangle. The treasure is buried in a box or chest.

Dots. Treasure is buried in a cave or caves as indicated by the number of dots.

Triangle with dot in center. The treasure is buried in the center of a triangle formed by trees or rocks.

Shaft and steps. The treasure is buried down a shaft or in a cave.

Three wavy lines. This sign indicates that the treasure is buried near a stream or that a stream is to be crossed to reach the treasure.

Triangle with a long base. The treasure will be found at one side of a triangle marked by trees or rocks.

Triangle with a curve extending from one angle. The treasure is buried around a bend or curve from a triangle formed by trees or rocks.

Curve over a dot. Treasure is buried directly underneath.

Crescent. The treasure will be found in mountains.

Oro. This word means gold in Spanish and indicates that gold exists in the vicinity. The letter G is used sometimes with the same meaning.

This symbol indicates that the treasure is hidden in a tunnel or mine shaft.

36.

GUIDE TO HIDDEN TREASURE IN THE UNITED STATES AND ITS WATERS

SUNKEN SHIPS

SUNKEN SHIPS literally cover the bottom of the navigable waters of the world, and practically every one has taken some treasure down with it.

The list of sunken ships below consists only of those that have been lost in the inland waters of the United States or in the coastal waters of the continental United States, and that are known to have carried considerable treasure. The approximate location and date of the sinking, as well as the estimated value of the cargo the ship was carrying, are shown wherever this information is available.

CALIFORNIA

Off Cortes Bank: Unidentified Spanish galleon, 1717, $700,000.
Off Crescent City: American steamer *Brother Jonathan*, 1865, $800,000.
Owens Lake: Unidentified treasure ship.
Off Point Arguello: American steamer *Yankee Blade*, 1854, $2,000,000.
Sacramento River: American steamer *Belle*, 1865, $100,000.
Off San Francisco: American steamer *Río de Janeiro*, 1901, $6,000,000.
San Francisco Bay: American steamer *R. J. Cochrane*, 1911, $96,000.
Off San Miguel Island: Unidentified Spanish galleon.
Off San Nicolas Island: Unidentified Spanish galleon.
Santa Barbara Channel: Spanish galleon *San Sebastian*, $2,000,000.
Off Santa Catalina Island: Unidentified Spanish galleon, 1598, $2,000,000.
  (off Ship's Rock): Unidentified Spanish frigate, 1852, $1,200,000.
Monterey Bay (Stillwater Cove): Unidentified Spanish galleon.
Wilmington Harbor: American steamer *Ada Hancock*, 1863, $40,000.

CONNECTICUT

Off Bridgeport: American steamer *Lexington*.
Off New London: Unidentified Spanish galleon.
Off Stonington: American frigate *Defense*, 1779, $500,-000.

DELAWARE

Off Lewes: British frigate *De Braak*, 1798, $15,000,000.
Off Rehoboth: British frigate *Faithful Steward*, 1785, $500,000.

FLORIDA

Apalachee Bay: Unidentified privateer, $5,000,000.
Apalachicola Bay: Unidentified American frigate, 1819, $200,000.
Carysfort Reef: 14 unidentified Spanish galleons, 1715, $63,500,000.
Charlotte Harbor: Gasparilla's pirate craft, $5,000,000.
Choctawhatchee Bay: 12 unidentified pirate ships.
Off Duck Key: Unidentified Spanish galleon.
Off Fort Lauderdale: Unidentified Spanish galleon.
Off Fort Pierce: Unidentified treasure ship.
Off Gasparilla Island: Gasparilla's pirate ship, 1821, $1,000,000.
Off Key West: Spanish galleon *Santa Rosa*, $35,000,000.
Off Pigeon Key: Unidentified schooner, $5,000,000.
Off St. Bernard Bay: 5 unidentified Spanish galleons, 1767, $6,000,000.
Off Soldier's Key: Unidentified British frigate, 1829, $2,000,000.
Steinhatchee River: Unidentified Confederate ship, $500,000.
Suwannee River: Unidentified Spanish schooner.
  (mouth): Unidentified pirate craft, $5,000,000.
Off Vero Beach: Spanish galleon *Santa Margarita*, 1595, $7,000,000.

MASSACHUSETTS

Off Highland Light: American steamer *Portland,* 1898, $200,000.

Off Lovell's Island, Boston Harbor: French warship *Magnifique,* 1782.

Near Nantucket Shoals Light: American steamer *Oregon,* 1944, $8,000,000; American steamer *Republic,* 1909, $3,000,000.

Off Orleans: Pirate ship *Whydah,* 1717, $100,000.

MICHIGAN

Off Alpena: American steamer *Pewabic,* 1865, $200,-000.

Off East Tawas: American schooner *Kitty Reeves,* 1870, $250,000.

Off Escanaba: Unidentified ship, $4,500,000.

Off Harbor Beach: American steamer *R. G. Coburn,* 1871, $185,000.

In Lake Erie off Monroe: American steamer *Lexington,* 1846, $300,000.

Off Manitou Islands: American steamer *Templeton.*

Saginaw Bay: American schooner *Fay,* $200,000.

Near Straits of Mackinac: La Salle's ship *Griffon,* 1679; American steamer *Westmoreland,* $100,000.

NEW JERSEY

Off Cape May: American steamer *City of Athens,* $3,000,000; unidentified Spanish galleon, $5,000,-000.

Delaware Channel: British frigate *Augusta,* 1777, $1,000,000; British frigate *Merlin,* 1777, $2,000,-000.

Off Ocean City: Unidentified Spanish galleon.

NEW YORK

Off Buffalo: American steamer *Anthony Wayne,* 1850, $100,000.

Between Buffalo and Dunkirk: American steamer *Dean Richmond,* 1893, $30,000.

Off Dunkirk: American steamer *Erie,* 1841, $100,000.

Between Dunkirk and Erie, Pa.: American steamer *Atlantic,* 1852, $60,000; American steamer *City of Detroit,* 1873, $200,000.

East River: British warship *Hussar,* 1780, $5,000,000; British warship *Lexington,* 1780, $1,800,000.

Long Island Sound: American brigantine *Vineyard,* 1830, $54,000.

NEBRASKA

Missouri River near Blair: American steamer *Bertrand,* 1862, $100,000.

NORTH CAROLINA

Off Cape Hatteras: American steamer *Central America,* 1857, $3,000,000; American steamer *Kensington,* 1871; American steamer *Pulaski,* 1838; American steamer *Santiago,* 1924.

Off Nags Head: American steamer *Huron,* 1877.

Off Wrightsville Beach: Confederate ship *Fannie & Jennie,* 1864.

OHIO

Off Sandusky: American steamer *G. R. Griffin,* 1896.

OREGON

Columbia River Bar off Coos Bay: American schooner *Sunshine,* 1875, $28,000.

TEXAS

Off Brazos Santiago: American steamer *Clara Woodhouse,* 1877, $80,000; American steamer *Ida Lewis,* 1875, $20,000; French brigantine *Reine des Mers,* 1875, $100,000; American schooner *Texas Ranger,* 1875, $200,000.

(vicinity): American steamer *S. J. Lee,* 1873, $100,-000.

Lavaca River mouth (near Lolita): Unidentified pirate craft.

Matagorda Bay: Spanish frigate *Santa Rosa,* 1816, $2,000,000.

Off Padre Island: Cortéz galleon; American steamer *Fleeta,* 1874, $30,000; American steamer *Paisano,* 1875, $200,000; French bark *Maria Theresa,* 1880, $100,000; 16 unidentified Spanish galleons, 1552; unidentified Spanish galleon, 1811, $500,-000.

Rio Grande mouth (near Brownsville): American steamer *Jessie,* 1875, $100,000.

(off Rio Grande City): American steamer *Carrie A. Thomas,* 1880, $125,000.

VIRGINIA

Off Virginia Capes: American steamer *Merida,* 1911, $5,500,000.

WISCONSIN

Wisconsin River: Unidentified river boat, $100,000.

LOST MINES IN THE UNITED STATES

ANY COMPREHENSIVE LIST of lost mines must include many whose origins are a mixture of fact and fiction. The following list, believed to be the most complete ever published, contains some mines whose existence is undoubtedly based upon legend, but on the other hand there is no doubt that legend often has its roots in fact.

The approximate locations of these lost mines are based upon the best information available and on some twenty years of research. In most cases only a general area can be indicated, and even then there is room for argument.

ARIZONA

Apache County (northern): Lost Shoemaker Mine, Lost Black Burro Mine (or northern Navajo County)

Arivapai Hills northwest of Tucson: Yuma's Lost Mine

Baboquivari Mountains: Lost Trooper's Mine

Cerro Colorado Mountains northeast of Nogales: Lost Blonde Mayo Mine

Cochise County: Sandstone Lost Mine, Old Papago's Lost Mine (or southern Santa Cruz County)

(southeastern): Lost Mine of the Guadalupes, Lost Virgin Guadalupe Mine

(southern): Geronimo's Lost Mine, Lost San Pedro Mine, Lost Shepherd's Mine

(western): Cienega Benders Lost Mine (or eastern Pima County)

Coconino County (northern): Lost Monument Valley Mine

(southwestern): Coconino Lost Mine, Lost Padre Mine

Estrella Mountains southwest of Phoenix: Lost Joaquin Campoy Mine

Four Peaks country northeast of Phoenix: Black Maverick Lost Mine

Colorado River (vicinity of Navajo Bridge): John D. Lee's Lost Mine

Gila County (northwestern): Miner's Lost Mine, Lost Tonto Trail Mine

(northern Sierra Ancha Mountains): Sander's Lost Mine

(southern): Cibicue Apaches' Lost Mine, Lost Mine of Hat Mountains, Lost Six-Shooter Mine

Maricopa County: Lost Adams Diggings

(southern): Lost Soldier Mine

(vicinity of Wickenburg): Negro Ben's Lost Mine

Mogollon Mountains: Lost Mine of the Mogollons

Mohave County (vicinity of Topock): Lost Nugget Mine

Navajo County (northern): Lost Black Burro Mine (or Apache County)

Pajarita Mountains near Nogales: Lost Mine of Cerro Ruido

Phoenix (northeast, in Four Peaks country): Black Maverick Lost Mine

(about 40 miles west of): Lost Squaw Hollow Mine

Pima County (eastern): Cienega Benders Lost Mine (or western Cochise County)

(vicinity of Arivaca): Lost Sopari Mine

(northeast of Arivaca): Lost Mine of the Cerro Colorado

(San Cayetano Mountains): Lost Mine of San Cayetano

(southern): Lost Mine of Baboquivari Mountains, Lost Clark Silver Mine

(southwestern): Lost Tenhachape Mine, Waggoner's Lost Mine

(south of Tucson): Lost Esmeralda Mine, Lost Mine of Old Guevavi

(western): Lost Mine of the Ajo Mountains, Lost Jabonero Mine

Santa Catalina Mountains south of Oracle: Lost Escalante Mine (Mine with the Iron Door)

Santa Cruz County (southern): Lost Planchas de Plata Mine, Old Papago's Lost Mine (or Cochise County)

(western): Lost Mine of Tumacacori

Superstition Mountains: Lost Bear Hunter's Mine, Doc Thorne's Lost Mine, Lost Don Miguel Peralta Mine, Lost Dutchman Mine

Tascosa Range south of Tucson: Lost Mine of Carreta Canyon

Yavapai County (vicinity of Congress Junction): Lost Mine of the Golden Cup (Caugh Oir)

(northeastern): Old Mose's Lost Dutch Oven Mine

(near Sycamore Springs): Lost Nigger Ben Mine

Yuma County (Adonde Range): Lost Squaw Mine

(Eagle Tail Mountains): Lost Frenchman Mine

(northwestern): Lost Cowboy Mine

(vicinity of Quartzsite): Quartzsite Lost Mine

(vicinity of Salome): Lost Glory Hole Mine

(Sierra Pinta Mountains, southeastern): Lost Dry Washer Mine

(southern): Lost Shepherd Girl Mine

(western): Lost Indian Placer Mine, Major Peeples Lost Mine

ARKANSAS

Montgomery County vicinity: Lost Spanish Silver Mine

Ouachita County area: Lost Spanish Mine

Ozark Mountains: Aztec Lost Mine

Searcy County vicinity: De Soto's Lost Silver Mine, Hermit Tabor's Lost Mine

Scott County (vicinity of Waldron): Lost Louisiana Gold Mine

Sevier County (Gillham region): Lost Mine of the Cosatot

Yell County (vicinity of Dardanelle): Lost Caddo Indian Mine

CALIFORNIA

Death Valley: Lost Arch Mine, Lost Bob Black Mine, Lost Chicken Bone Mine, Lost Mine of Colorado Canyon, Gomer Richards' Lost Mine

(Funeral Range): Lost Gunsight Mine

(Panamint Range): Breyfogle Lost Mine

Eldorado County: Lost Sonora Ledge Mine

(Diamond Valley region): Snowshoe Thompson's Lost Mine

Kern County: Old Schippe's Lost Mine

(Randsburg region): Goller's Lost Mine

(Tehachapi Mountains): Lost Mine of Frazier Park

Los Angeles County (southern): Lost Mine of Mt. Disappointment

Marin County: Golden Gate Lost Mine

Mono County: Whiteman's Lost Mine

(vicinity of Mono Lake): Lost Cement Mine

Nevada County (Nevada City area): Lost Padre Mine

Plumas County: Lingard's Lost Lake of Gold, Stoddard's Lake of Gold (or Sierra County)

Riverside County: Lost French Bullring Mine, Lost Schwartz Mine (or San Diego County)

San Bernardino County: Lost Ace in the Hole Mine, Adams Lost Mine, Old Man Lee's Lost Mine, Straying Burro Lost Mine, Lost Tub Mine

(Alvord Mountains): Alvord's Lost Mine

(Amboy region): Lost Amboy Mine

(Clipper Mountains): Lost Dutch Oven Mine

(Ivanpah Mountains): Lost Mine of Kokoweef Mountain

(San Bernardino Mountains): Lost Mine of Granite Mountain, Lost Mine of Minnelusa Canyon

(Sheep Hole Mountains): Lost Shotgun Mine

(southeastern): Lost Clothes Line Mine

(southwestern): Lost Mine of Van Duzen Canyon

(north of Twentynine Palms): Lost Mine of the Bullion Mountains

San Diego County: Lost Black Crow Mine, Lost Gray Phantom Mine, Lost Nigger Jim Mine, Pegleg Smith's Lost Mine, Lost Phantom Mine, Pierre Hausenberger's Lost Mine

(Fish Mountains): Lost Portuguese Mine

(Borego Springs vicinity): Old Hank's Lost Mine

(Chocolate Mountains): Black Butte Lost Mine, Pegleg Smith II's Lost Mine

(Cocopah Mountains): Lost Mine of Jesus Arroa

(eastern): Yaqui Lost Mine

(or Riverside County): Lost Schwartz Mine

(Ramona region): Lost El Cajon Mine (also known as the Lost Wadham and the Lost Barona)

(Santa Rosa Mountains): Lost Emerald Mine

San Luis Obispo County: Lost Chinaman Mine, Lost Priest Mine

Shasta County: Lost Cabin Mine of Soda Creek

(Redding region): Old Man Waite's Lost Mine

Sierra County: Lost Mine of Kanaka Creek Canyon

(Downieville area): Castle Ravine Lost Mine

(or Plumas County): Stoddard's Lake of Gold

Tulare County (Sequoia National Park area): Lost Pipe Clay Mine

Yuba County (Marysville region): Lost River of Gold Mine

COLORADO

Southcentral: White's Lost Cement Mine

Alamosa County (San Luis Valley region): Juan Carlos Lost Mine

Huerfano County: Breckinridge Huntsman Lost Mine

(southern): Lost Mine of Wet Mountain Valley, Spanish Peaks Lost Mine (and Western Las Animas County)

Las Animas County: Lost Mine of Las Animas Valley, Pierre's Lost Mine

(southern): Whatoyah Lost Mine

(Spanish Peaks region): Lost Mine of Marble Mountain

(western): Spanish Peaks Lost Mine

La Plata County (La Plata Mountains): Lost Josephine Mine

Mesa County (Grand Junction region): Lost Pin Gold Mine

Mineral County (Creede region): Lost Mine of Treasure Mountain

(region): Lost Mine of Hick's Mountain

Moffat County (northwestern): Lost Phantom Mine

IDAHO

Bonneville County (Idaho Falls region): Lost Trail Creek Mine

Camas County (Corral area): Lost Sheepherder's Mine

Clark County: Goddard & Tyler's Lost Mine, Lost Texas Jack Mine

(Spencer region): Lost Tenderfoot Mine

Custer County (Salmon River Mountains): Swimm's Lost Mine

Lemhi County: Lost Cleveland Mine, Hahn's Lost Mine

Idaho County (eastern): Lost Basin Mine

LOUISIANA

Calcasieu Parish: Lost Mine of Wyndham Creek

MAINE

Hancock County: Lost Mine of Lead Mountain

MICHIGAN

Ontonagon County: Lost Mine of Silver City

MISSOURI

Douglas County area: Lost Spain Silver Mine

Hickory County: Lost Brooksie Mine

Stone County (vicinity of Galena): Lost Spanish Mine

MONTANA

Garfield County (vicinity of Piney Buttes): Lost Keyes Mine

(Mosby region): Lost Indian Gold Mine

Gallatin Range: Lost Rea Mine (Gallatin or Park county)

Lake County: Lost Springer Mine

Lewis and Clark County (vicinity of Helena): Lost Keise Mine

Phillips County: Lost Neepee Mine

NEVADA

Churchill County (Stillwater Mountains): Lost Chicken Craw Mine

Clark County: Lost Devil's Peak Mine, Lost Nelots Mine

(Las Vegas area): Lost Diamond Mine

(vicinity of Searchlight): Lost Skillet of Gold Mine

Douglas County (Pine Nut Range): Cody Lost Mine

Humboldt County: Lost Tenderfoot Mine, Lost Three Lakes of Gold, Lost Padre Mine

(Black Rock Desert area): Hardin's Lost Black Rock Mine

(Black Rock Range): Lost Mine of the Little Brown Men

Lincoln County (southwestern): Lost Doublecross Mine

Mineral County: Lost Mormon Mine

(eastern, Cedar Mountains): Lost Cedars Mine

Nye County (southern): Lost Stovepipe Mine

Storey County (Virginia City area): Lost Grosch Silver Mine

Washoe County: Lost Pick and Shovel Mine

(southern): Lost Cave of Gold, Lost Golden Eagle Mine

NEW HAMPSHIRE

Carroll County (vicinity of Whittier): Lost Mine of Ossipee Range

NEW MEXICO

East central: De Gavilan's Lost Mine

Catron County (Mogollon Mountains): Lost Waterfall Mine

Grant County: Lost Adams Mine, Snively Lost Diggings, Lost White's Cement Mine
Otero County (Guadalupe Mountains): Lost Sublette Mine
  (region): Lost Mica Mine
Sangre de Cristo Mountains (Taos or Colfax county region): Lost La Mina Perdida Mine

NEW YORK

Adirondack Mountains: Mt. Colden Lost Mine, Adolphus Lavigne Lost Mine, Lost Silver Mine of Nippleton
Catskill Mountains: Lost Mine of Teunis
Dunderburg Mountain area: Lost Tinker Mine
Schoharie County: Blenheim Lost Silver Mine

NORTH CAROLINA

Cherokee County (vicinity of Andrews): Lost Indian Silver Mine

NORTH DAKOTA

Stark County (vicinity of Belfield): Dr. Dibb Lost Mine

OKLAHOMA

Haskell County: Lost Standing Rock Mine

OREGON

Southeastern Oregon or northwestern Nevada: Lost Blue Bucket Mine
Jackson County (Jacksonville area): Missing Indian Lost Mine
  (vicinity of Rogue River): Ed Schieffelin's Lost Mine
Malheur County: Lost Malheur Mine
Wallowa Mountains (northeastern): Lost Bear Creek Mine

SOUTH DAKOTA

Black Hills region: Lost Cabin Mine, Lost Mine of Signal Mountain

TEXAS

Big Bend country south of Sanderson in Terrell or Brewster county: Lost Seminole Bill Mine
Brewster County: (Chisos Mountains): Lost Mine of the Phantom Mountains
Corpus Christi vicinity: Lost Villareal Silver Mine
Culberson County (Guadalupe Mountains): Lost Sublette Mine

Franklin Mountain near El Paso: Lost Padre Mine
Lavaca County (vicinity of Hallettsville): Lost Dutchman Mine
Lee County (Giddings region): Goacher's Lost Mine
Llano County: Lost Blanco Mine
Llano River vicinity (northwest of San Antonio): Lost San Saba Mine (also known as Lost Bowie Mine, Lost Almagres Mine, Lost Las Amarillas, and Lost La Mina de las Iguanas)
Nueces River region (southern Texas): Lost Spanish Nueces Mine
Paisano Pass vicinity (Brewster or Presidio County): Engineer's Lost Mine
Panhandle country: Lost Mine of Lighthouse Canyon

UTAH

Grand County: Lost Caleb Rhodes Mine
Juab County: Mammoth Miner Lost Mine
Millard County: Margum Pass Lost Mine
San Juan County area: Pedros Lost Mine
  (Montecillo area): Lost Pot Holes Mine
Tooele County: Lost Brigham Young Mine, Lost Crossland Mine
Uintah County region: Lost Ewing Mine
Utah County (near Spanish Fork): Lost Nephite Mine
Washington County (vicinity of St. George): Lost Santa Clara Mine

VERMONT

Rutland County (vicinity of Pittsford): Lost Birch Hill Silver Mine

VIRGINIA

Wise and Dickenson counties vicinity: Lost Mine of Passage Creek Gap

WASHINGTON

Asotin County (junction of Grande Ronde and Snake rivers): Lost Shovel Creek Mine
Cowlitz County region: Lost Mine of Ostrander Creek

WYOMING

Albany County (vicinity of Centennial): Lost Docony Mine
Big Horn County: Lost Dutchman Mine, Lost Shovel Mine
Big Horn Mountains near source of Crazy Woman Creek: Lost Cabin Mine
Carbon County (Sierra Madre Mountains): Lost Old Shoe Mine
Natrona County (northwestern): Lost Soldier Mine

BURIED TREASURE GUIDE TO THE UNITED STATES

THE FOLLOWING BURIED TREASURES are all located within the continental boundaries of the United States and include all treasures other than lost mines and sunken ships. Although the existence of most of these treasures is based upon some documentary evidence or historical fact, some are legendary in origin. Even legend, however, often has a forgotten background in fact, and a number of treasures, long considered legendary have been found.

The locations of these treasures although based on many years of painstaking research, can only be approximate. It is a challeng to the treasure hunter to go out and pinpoint them more precisely.

ALABAMA

Baldwin County (Bay Minette): Unidentified pirate treasure
  (Mobile Point): Pirate treasure of old Fort Morgan
  (along Perdido Bay): Treasure of Nunez Ferry
Elmore (Tallassee County): Civil War treasure
Mobile County (Bayou Labatre): Lafitte's treasure
Pickens County (Gordo): Iron treasure chest
Tallapoosa County (Dadeville): Civil War treasure
Elmore and Tallapoosa counties: Civil War treasure

ARIZONA

Border area of southern Arizona: Don Padriac's lost mission treasure
Cochise County (Chiricahua Mountains): Skeleton Canyon bandit treasure
  (Wildcat Canyon, Chiricahua Mountains): Blackjack Ketchum's bandit treasure
  (Tombstone): Flooded treasure of Tombstone
Coconino County (Flagstaff): Roy Gardner's train robbery treasure
  (San Francisco Peaks area): Lost treasure of the Padres
Maricopa County (Bradshaw Mountains): Treasure of Horse Thief Basin
  (Estrella Mountains): Joaquín Campoy's cave treasure
  (Wickenburg): Treasure of Walnut Grove Dam
Navajo County (Holbrook): Treasure of the Turquoise Shrine
Pima County (Ajo Mountains): Montezuma's buried treasure
  (Tucson): San Xavier del Bac Mission treasure
  (Tumacacori National Monument): Treasure of Tumacacori
  (Vail): Colossal Cave bandit treasure
Santa Cruz County (Calabasas): Treasure of old Guevavi Mission
  (Tascosa Range): Lost treasure of Carreta Canyon
Yuma County (Cocopah Mountains): Jesus Arroa treasure
  (along Colorado River): Redondo Ruins treasure
  (La Paz): Treasure of Rancho Los Yumas
  (along Mexican border): Lost Mission of Tinajas Altas treasure
  (O'Nell Pass): Wagon train massacre treasure

ARKANSAS

Benton County: Spanish treasure cave
Chicot County (near Lake Chicot): Stuart's Island outlaw treasure
Crawford County: Buried treasure of White Mountain
Izard County (Pineville): Madre Vena Cave treasure
Pope County (Norristown Mountain near Russellville): The Lovely Brothers' treasure
Searcy County: De Soto's buried treasure
Washington County (Fayetteville): William Flynn's buried treasure

CALIFORNIA

Calaveras County (San Andreas): Joaquin Murietta's buried treasure
Death Valley: Burnt Wagons lost treasure, Tom Shannon's lost treasure
Imperial County (Kane Springs): Treasure ship of the desert
Lassen County (Janesville): Henry Gordier's Lost treasure
Los Angeles City: Lost treasure of Elysian Park Hills
Los Angeles County (Hollywood): Treasure of Cahuenga Pass
  (Manhattan Beach): Pirate treasure of Duncan Ranch
  (Norwalk): McNally Ranch lost treasure
Marin County: Buried treasure of Golden Point
Mariposa County: Lost treasure of Aqua Frio
Merced County: Treasure of Rancho Centinella
Monterey County (Monterey): Sir Francis Drake's treasure
Nevada County (Nevada City): Casserly's lost treasure
Pinnacles National Monument (San Benito and Monterey counties): Tiburcio Vasquez' treasure
Placer County (near Donner Lake): Donner Party treasure
San Bernardino County (Calico): Pat Hogan's buried treasure, Hidden treasure of Gifford Gardens
San Diego County: Carrizo Wash Stage holdup treasure, San Felipe Stage Station treasure, Lost treasure of Santa Isabel, Signal Hill lost treasure
  (border area): Lost Jacumba treasure
  (Borego Desert): Bluebeard Watson's buried treasure
  (Borego Valley): Treasure of the burnt wagons
  (Carrizo Hills): Joaquín Murietta's buried treasure
  (vicinity of San Luis Rey Mission): Cortéz treasure of San Luis Rey
  (Vallecito): Vallecito stage treasure
San Francisco Bay area: Martin Thierry's pirate treasure
San Luis Obispo County (San Luis Obispo): Cave Landing buried treasure, Robber's Cave treasure
Santa Clara County (San Jose): Treasure of Rancho Teresa
Shasta County (Shasta): Joaquín Murietta's buried treasure
Trinity Mountains (Trinity or Shasta county): Rattlesnake Dick's bandit treasure
Tuolumne County (Columbia): Buried treasure of Tom Davis
Yuba County (Camptonville): Billy Snyder's buried treasure

COLORADO

Archuleta County (Pagosa Springs): Treasure Mountain buried gold
Bent County (Las Animas): Buried treasure of Bent's Fort

Garfield County (Grand Valley): Bandit treasure of Grand Valley

Huerfano County: Spanish Peaks buried treasure (or Las Animas County)

Lake County (Leadville): Baby Doe's buried treasure

Larimer County (Ft. Collins): Buried treasure of Natural Fort, Lost treasure of Robber's Roost

Las Animas County (Purgatory River area): Lost treasure of Purgatory Canyon

(or Huerfano County): Spanish Peaks buried treasure

Saguache County (northwest of Saguache): Buried treasure of Round Mountain

Sedgwick County (Julesburg): Italian's Cave buried treasure

CONNECTICUT

Clarke's Island in Connecticut River: Whisking Clarke's buried treasure

Fairfield County (Stratford Point near Milford): Captain Kidd's treasure

Fisher's Island, N. Y., off Mystic: Fisher's Island buried treasure

Goose Island off Norwalk: Goose Island treasure

Hartford County (Wethersfield): Captain Kidd's treasure chests

(near Wethersfield): Kidd's treasure at Tyron's landing

New London County (Lyme): Captain Kidd's treasure

Off Norwalk: Pirate treasure of Sheffield Islands

Thimbles Islands (Money Island): Kidd's buried treasure

(Thimble Island): Kidd's treasure

DELAWARE

Kent County (Bombay Hook Island): Captain Kidd's treasure

New Castle County (Blackbird Creek area): Blackbeard's buried treasure

DISTRICT OF COLUMBIA

Washington, D.C.: Treasure of the Marine Corps House

FLORIDA

Anclote Key: Unidentified pirate treasure

Near Caesar's Creek: Black Caesar's treasure

Charlotte Harbor: Treasure of Carlos of the Calusas

Choctawhatchee Bay area: Billy Bowlegs' buried treasure

Clay County (Green Cove Springs): Spanish buried treasure

Dade County (Miami): Pirate treasure of Coconut Grove

(North Miami): Pirate treasure

(Ojus): Pirate treasure on Snake Creek

Dixie County (Cross City): Bahama Trader's treasure

Duval County (Mayport): Pirate treasure

Elliot Key: Pirate treasure

Escambia County (Pensacola): Pirate treasure chests

(near Pensacola): Spanish Cove treasure

Everglades region: Confederate treasure

Fernandina Harbor: Captain Kidd's treasure

Franklin County (Money Bayou near Apalachicola): Pirate Copeland's treasure

Grassy Key: Buried Mexican treasure

Hillsborough County: Treasure of Turtle Mound

(Plant City): Pirate treasure

(Tampa): Gasparilla's Cave treasure

Key Largo: Pirate treasure

Near Key West: Black Caesar's treasure

Lake Okeechobee (St. Lucie Inlet): Ashley gang bandit treasure

Marion County (Ocala): Spanish buried treasure

(Silver Springs): De Soto's buried treasure

Monroe County (Boca Chica): Pirate Demons' treasure

Nassau County (near Fernandina): Amelia Island pirate treasure

Old Matecumbe Key: Pirate treasure

Palm Beach County (Boca Raton): Blackbeard's buried treasure

Panther Key: Gasparilla pirate treasure

Pigeon Key: Pirate treasure

St. Johns County (St. Augustine): Richard Crowe's buried treasure

Sanibel Island: Black Caesar's treasure

Shark River area: John Rackham's pirate treasure

Siesta Key: Pirate treasure

Suwannee River: Gasparilla's treasure ship

(mouth): Pirate treasure of Fowler's Bluff

(region): Bumble Bee Island treasure

Volusia County: Ponce de Léon's buried treasure

Wakulla County (St. Marks): Lewis Leland's pirate treasure

GEORGIA

Baldwin County (Milledgeville): Treasure of the Peter Williams' house

Blackbeard's Island in Sapelo Sound: Blackbeard's buried treasure

Chatham County (Savannah): Flint House pirate treasure

Ossabaw Island: Blackbeard's pirate treasure

Tallulah Falls (Haversham and Rabun counties): Cole Rogers' treasure

IDAHO

Ada County (Boise): Bandit treasure, Buried treasure of Rocky Canyon

Bannock County (McCammon): McCammon Stage robbery treasure

Bingham County (Blackfoot): Lava fields buried treasure

Boise County (Idaho City) Stage robbery treasure

Butte County (Arco): Stolen pack train treasure

(Root Hog Divide): Highwayman's treasure

Cassia County (Oakley): City of Rocks bandit treasure

Clark County (Lidy Hot Springs): Buried bandit treasure

Craters of the Moon National Monument: Bandit treasure

Fremont County (Rea): Bandit treasure

(Teton Basin): Stage holdup treasure

Gem County: Brown's Bench treasure

Idaho County (Florence): Pack train treasure

Jefferson County: Camas Creek bandit treasure, Camas Stage robbery treasure
(Heise): Buried treasure of Kelly Canyon
Lemhi County: Birch Creek Stage robbery treasure
(Leadore): Stolen stage treasure

ILLINOIS

Clinton County: Treasure of John Hill's Fort
Cook County (Chicago): John Hoffman treasure
Hardin County: Cave-in-Rock treasure

INDIANA

Huntington County: Silver Creek treasure
Jackson County (Seymour): Train robbery treasure
Martin County (Shoals): Absalom Fields' buried treasure
Perry County (Cannelton): Lafayette's lost treasure
Spencer County (Rockport): River boat treasure

IOWA

Dubuque County (Dubuque): Kelly's Bluff treasure

KANSAS

Clark County (Ashland): Treasure of Big Basin
Edwards County (Offerle): Buried '49ers' treasure
Ford County (Dodge City): Coronado's buried treasure, Mexican wagon train treasure
Graham County (Morland): Buried Spanish treasure
Morton County (Elkhart): Point of Rocks bandit treasure
Nemaha County (Seneca): Nemaha River treasure

KENTUCKY

Southeastern Kentucky: John Swift's buried treasure
Fayette County (Lexington): Alleghan Hall treasure, the Coldstream Stud treasure
Floyd County (Hueysville): Jack Neal's buried treasure
Greenup County (Greenup): Indian cave treasure
McCracken County (Paducah): James Langstaff's treasure
Webster County (Dixon): Harpes Head Road treasure

LOUISIANA

Louisiana-Texas border: Lafitte's treasure on Sabine River
Ascension Parish (Galvez Town): Lafitte's treasure
Barataria Bay area: Johnny Gambi's buried treasure
(Calillan Island): Lafitte's treasure
Calcasieu Parish (Lake Charles): Lafitte's treasure at Contraband Bayou
Grant Parish: Robber's treasure of Hull Lake
(Selma): Gold Miner's buried treasure
Iberia Parish: Lafitte's Jefferson Island treasure
Lake Borgne: Lafitte's treasure
Ouachita Parish: Old Camp Place buried treasure
Pointe Coupee Parish (New Roads): Parlange Plantation buried treasure
Red River Parish (Coushatta): Red River treasure
St. James Parish: Treasure of Valcour Aime
(Lutcher): Buried Indian treasure
(St. Joseph): Lake plantation treasure

St. John the Baptist Parish: D'Estrahan plantation treasure, the buried treasure of St. Rose
St. Landry Parish: Grand Coteau buried treasure
(Opelousas): Lost treasure of Chretien Point
St. Martin Parish: Narcisse Thibodeaux's treasure
St. Tammany Parish: Buried treasure of Honey Island Swamp
Terrebonne Bay: Buried treasure of Caillou Island
Vermilion Parish: Lafitte's Pecan Island treasure

MAINE

Boothbay Harbor: Kidd's Squirrel Island treasure
(Outer Hebron Island): Pirate treasure
Casco Bay (Bailey Island): Pirate treasure
(Cliff Island): Captain Kieff's pirate treasure, Captain Kidd's pit treasure
(Cushing Island): Dixie Bull's pirate treasure
(Great Chebeague Island): Pirate treasure
(Jewell's Island): Captain Kidd's treasure
(Pond Island): Lowe's pirate treasure
Finley Creek area: Pirate treasure chest
Hancock County (Castine): Baron Castine's treasure
Isle au Haut: Kidd's Money Cove treasure
Kennebec County (Hallowell): Captain Kidd's treasure
(Pittston): Captain Kidd's treasure
Lincoln County (Edgecomb): Samuel Trask's buried treasure
Monhegan Island: Captain Kidd's buried treasure
Penobscot Bay area: Buried treasure of Codlead Marsh
(Musselridge Channel): Captain Kidd's treasure
Penobscot River area, lower: Captain Kidd's treasure
Richmond's Island: Buried pirate treasure
Sheepscot River in vicinity of Wiscasset: Captain Kidd's treasure chest
Waldo County (Frankfort): Captain Kidd's treasure
(Liberty): Timothy Barrett's treasure
Washington County (Machias): Pirate Bellamy's buried treasure

MARYLAND

Baltimore: Mansion House treasure
Baltimore County (Catonsville): Jean Champlaigne's treasure
Frederick County (Frederick): Hagen's Tavern buried treasure
Miles River area (eastern shore): Goldsborough Creek treasure
St. Marys County (California): Resurrection Mansion treasure
Tred Avon River region (eastern shore): Tred Avon treasure
Watts Creek area (eastern shore): Jake's Hole buried treasure
Wicomico County: Patty Cannon's buried treasure

MASSACHUSETTS

Barnstable County (Oyster Harbors): Pirate treasure
(Provincetown): Buried treasure of Money Hill
Berkshire County: Buried treasure of the Hessians
(Cheshire): Captain Kidd's treasure
(Dalton): Sand Mill buried treasure

(Greylock Mountain): Hermit's buried treasure
(Mt. Washington area): Black Grocery gang treasure
Boston Bay (Apple Island): William Marsh's buried treasure
(Calf Island): Pirate treasure
(Castle Island): Pirate treasure
(Conant's Island): Captain Kidd's treasure
(Deer Island): Money Bluff buried treasure
(Grape Island): Captain Billie's lost treasure
(Great Brewster Island): Pirate treasure
(Little Brewster Island): Pirate treasure
(Snake Island): John Quelch's pirate treasure
(Swan Island): John Breed's buried treasure
Cape Cod region: Chatham treasure chest
East Chop Light vicinity: Walker's pirate treasure
Essex County (Byfield): Pirate treasure
(Hog Island): Captain Kidd's treasure
(Lynn): Tom Veal's buried treasure
(Methuen): Daddy Frye's Hill treasure
(Plum Island): Harry Main's buried treasure
Franklin County (Turner's Falls): Captain Kidd's treasure
Hampshire County (West Chesterfield): Alden Culver buried treasure
Middlesex County (Wilmington): Devil's Den buried treasure
(Somerville): Brink's robbery treasure
Naushon Island: Buried treasure of Tarpaulin Cove
Suffolk County (Winthrop): Buried treasure of Shirley Point, Willard's Taproom treasure, Captain's buried treasure

MICHIGAN

Berrien County (Benton Harbor): House of David treasure
Drummond Island: British treasure of Fort Drummond
Espanore Island: Pirate treasure
Presque Isle County (Presque Isle): Francis Fontenoy's treasure

MINNESOTA

Pipestone County (Pipestone): James Boys' treasure
Sibley County (Henderson): Treasure of Charles Ney

MISSISSIPPI

Adams County (Natchez): Devil's Punchbowl treasure, Pirate treasure, White Horse Tavern treasure
Calhoun County (Calhoun City): Gore's buried treasure
Claiborne County (Rocky Springs): Mason gang treasure
Greene County (McLain): Spanish treasure
Hancock County (Bay St. Louis): Pirate House buried treasure
(Catahoula Swamp): Copeland gang treasure
Harrison County (Biloxi): Patrick Scott's buried treasure
(Pass Christian): Captain Dane's lost treasure
Sunflower County (Doddsville): Civil War treasure
Warren County (Blakely): John Murrell's buried treasure

MISSOURI

Southwestern Missouri: Spanish pirate treasure
Christian County: Lost Spanish treasure
McDonald County: Buried treasure of Bear Holler
Pulaski County: Lost treasure of Possum Ledge
St. Louis vicinity: Bandit treasure

MONTANA

Big Horn Mountains region: Lost cabin buried treasure
Granite County (Drummond): Lost treasure of Chinee Grade
Park County (Livingston): Buried stage robbery treasure
Phillips County (Malta): Kid Curry's buried treasure
Yellowstone County (Billings): Lost treasure of Horsethief Cache

NEBRASKA

Adams County (Hastings): Buried Indian treasure
Buffalo County (Kearney): Bank robbery treasure
Dawson County (Lexington): Highwayman's treasure
Knox County (Crofton): Outlaw treasure of Devil's Nest
Thurston County (Macy): Bandit treasure of Robber's Cave

NEVADA

Douglas County (Genoa): Genoa Stage holdup treasure
Mineral County (Belleville): Lost treasure of the Iron Flasks
(Columbus): Candaleria Mine lost treasure
Washoe County (vicinity of Pyramid Lake): Lost treasure of Pyramid Lake

NEW HAMPSHIRE

Grafton County (Campton): Treasure of the Worcester Cave
Hillsboro County (Merrimack): John Cromwell's buried treasure
(Rye Pond near Antrim): Captain Kidd's buried treasure
Isles of Shoals: Bluebeard's Smuttynose treasure, John Quelch's pirate treasure, Lost treasure of White Island
Rockingham County (Portsmouth): The Hemp Spinner's buried treasure, John Wentworth's treasure

NEW JERSEY

Atlantic City: Pirate treasure of Absecon Island
Burlington County (Burlington): Blackbeard's treasure
Cape May County (Cape May): Giles Shelly's buried treasure
Cape May region: Captain Kidd's treasure
(Turtle Bay): Joe Bradish pirate treasure
Essex County (Caldwell): Treasure of the murdered German officer
Hudson County (Homestead): Hendrick Dempster's treasure
Monmouth County: Treasure of the Pine Robbers
(Cliffwood): Captain Kidd's treasure

Ocean County (Island Beach): Treasure of the Bar-negat pirates

Salem County (Sharptown): Treasure of the Seven Star Tavern

NEW MEXICO

Northwestern New Mexico: Twenty tons of buried Mexican gold

Dona Ana County (San Andreas Mountains): The cave treasure of Dr. Noss

Eddy County: Lost Spanish treasure of Las Placitas

Lincoln County (Carrizo Hills): Mina del Toro treasure

McKinley County: Seven Cities of Cibola treasure

Otero County (Guadalupe Mountains): Buried Apache treasure

Torrance County: Buried treasure of Gran Quivira

Union County (southern): Lost treasure of Devoy's Peak

NEW YORK

Adirondack Mountains: Follingsby's lost treasure

Albany County (Knox): Robber's treasure of Wynd Cave

Annsville Creek region: Pirate treasure

Bear Mountain region: Letterrock Mountain treasure

Essex County (vicinity of Mt. Colden): British pay-master's lost treasure

(vicinity of Ticonderoga): Buried treasure of Lost Pond

Fisher's Island off Connecticut coast: Captain Kidd's treasure

Grand Island in Niagara River: Treasure of the Mad Frenchman

Green County (Palenville): Captain Kidd's Sleepy Hollow treasure

Isle Royal in St. Lawrence River: The French com-mander's treasure

Lake Champlain region: Lord Amherst treasure

Long Island: Charles Gibbs' pirate treasure

(Montauk Point): Joe Bradish pirate treasure

New York City: The Bobbit lost treasure

Orange County (vicinity of West Point): Captain Kidd's Crow's Nest treasure

(Kidd's Point on Hudson River, or Putnam County): Captain Kidd's treasure

Rockland County (Stony Point): Captain Kidd's Grassy Point treasure

Saratoga County (Saratoga Springs): General Bur-goyne's treasure

Schoharie County (Conesville): Captain Kidd's treas-ure

(South Gilboa): Buried pirate treasure

Washington County (Whitehall): Robert Gordon's buried treasure

Westchester County: Captain Kidd's treasure

(Money Hill): Joe Bradish pirate treasure

(Peekskill): Captain Kidd's treasure

NORTH CAROLINA

Beaufort County (Bath): Blackbeard's pirate treasure

(Plum Point): Blackbeard's treasure

Chatham County: Devil's Stamping Ground treasure

Chowan County (Edenton): Old Man Batt's buried treasure

Guilford County (High Point): Treasure of Brummel's Inn

New Hanover County: Stede Bonnett's pirate treasure

(Wilmington): Gander Hall treasure

(near Wrightsville Beach): Pirate treasure of Money Island

Ocracoke Island: Blackbeard's treasure

NORTH DAKOTA

Burke County: Big Butte lost treasure

Burleigh County (Bismarck): Buried treasure of Burnt Creek

McLean County (Garrison): Lost miner's buried gold

Slope County (Amidon): Lost treasure of Chalky Butte

Rolette County (Dunseith): Buried treasure of Turtle Mountain

OHIO

Logan County (Zanesfield): Buried British treasure

Preble County (Eaton): Bridge buried treasure

OKLAHOMA

Blaine County (Roman Nose State Park): Outlaw treas-ure

Caddo County (Cement): Buried Spanish treasure

Cimarron County (Kenton): Buried treasure of Black Mesa

Comanche County (Cache Creek area): Lost Govern-ment treasure

(Fort Sill): Camp Radziminski buried treasure

(Mount Scott): Buried Spanish treasure

(Seven Springs area): Buried Spanish treasure

(Twin Mountains area): Buried Spanish treasure

(Wichita Mountains): Jesse James treasure, Buried treasure of Cut Throat Gap

Creek County (Mannford): Dalton Gang treasure

Latimer County (Wilburton): Robber's Cave buried treasure

Le Flore County (Wister): Buried outlaw treasure

Tulsa County (Sand Springs): Dalton Gang treasure

OREGON

Hood River County: Lost treasure of Horse Thief Meadows

(Mount Hood): Bandit treasure of Laurel Hill

Jackson County: Buried treasure of the worried miners

Tillamook County (Manzanita): Pirate treasure of Neahkahnie Mountain

PENNSYLVANIA

Southwestern corner of Pennsylvania: General Brad-dock's buried treasure

Berks County: Doane Gang treasure

Delaware River: Lost Hessian gold

Northumberland County (Mt. Carmel): Treasure of the wrecked airliner

RHODE ISLAND

Block Island: Joe Bradish treasure, Captain Kidd's treasure

Canonicut Island: Captain Kidd's treasure

SOUTH CAROLINA

Berkeley County (on Santee River): Hampton House treasure

Horry County (Little River): Pirate treasure of Fort Randall

SOUTH DAKOTA

Black Hills region: Gordon Party lost treasure, Archie McLaughlin's treasure

  (Castle Creek): Lost treasure of the Four Crosses

  (Hat Creek): Lost Hat Creek treasure

  (Red Canyon): Metz family treasure

Codington County: Buried treasure of Long Lake

Custer County (Horse Thief Lake): Lame Johnnie's buried treasure

Hughes County (Pierre): Buried treasure of the Missouri, the Three Sisters' treasure

Lawrence County (Deadwood): The Four Directions treasure, Holy Terror Mine treasure

Pennington County (Pactola): Buried treasure of Burnt Ranch

  (Rapid City): Lost treasure of the Limestone Cave

TENNESSEE

Cocke County (Newport): Touhy Gang treasure

Cumberland County (Crossville): Indian silver cave treasure

Morgan County (Wartburg): Buried treasure of Big Clear Creek

TEXAS

Angelina County (Diboll): Treasure cannon of the Neches River

Arbuckle Mountains: Manuel Gomez' treasure

Bell County (Belton): Buried treasure of the Aguayo explorers

  (vicinity): Steinheimer's buried treasure

Bexar County (San Antonio area): Rondout train robbery treasure

Brewster County (Packsaddle Mountain): Buried Spanish treasure

Between Brownsville and Corpus Christi: Lost treasure of the Carreta Trail

Cameron County (Brownsville): Treasure of Lago de los Pajores, Buried treasure of Palo Alto

Castle Gap west of San Antonio: Maximilian's buried treasure

Cooke-Montague counties region: Old Spanish fort treasure

Corpus Christi region: Maximilian's buried treasure, Pirate treasure of Oso River, Jacob Ziegler's buried treasure (see also Nueces County)

Dimmit County: Lost Estambel Hill Treasure

Galveston vicinity: Lafitte's treasure at Virginia Point

Harris County (Humble): Marsh treasure of the Mexican convoy

Jeff Davis County: Lost treasure of Barrel Springs, Lost treasure of Deadman Springs

  (Davis Mountains): Red Curley's buried bandit treasure, Lost bandit treasure of Seminole Hill

Jefferson County: Pirate treasure of Sabine Pass

Kleberg County (Point of Rocks): Lafitte's buried treasure

LaSalle County: Lost treasure of the Sheep Pen Rocks

Lavaca River mouth: Lafitte's buried treasure

Live-Oak County: Paso Valeno buried treasure, Buried treasure of Round Lake

  (Annarose): José Ramírez buried treasure

  (Mikeska): Buried treasure of Paso Piedras

  (Three Rivers): Buried treasure of old Fort Merrill

Llano County (Llano): Buried treasure of Longhorn Cavern

McMullen County: Dan Dunham lost treasure, Spanish treasure of San Cajo Mountain, Lost treasure of the Laredo Crossing

Mustang Island: Lafitte's buried treasure

Nueces County (Corpus Christi): Fogg's buried treasure, Tontino's buried treasure chest

  (Flour Bluff): Lafitte's pirate treasure

Nueces River area: Lost Santa Ana treasure

  (above Corpus Christi): Lost treasure of the Casa Blanca

  (mouth near Corpus Christi): Pirate treasure

Padre Island: Lafitte's treasure, Mexican prospector's treasure, Wailing Wayne's lost treasure

  (southern): Singer family's buried treasure

Refugio County (Refugio): Pirate treasure of False Live Oak Point

St. Joseph's Island: Buried treasure of Vincent's Point

San Patricio County (Mathias): Buried treasure of Dobie Ranch

Stephens County (Breckenridge): Lost Mexican caravan treasure

Stonewall County (Aspermont): Lost Aztec Mission treasure

Taylor County: Buried treasure of Buffalo Gap

Val Verde County (Dorso): Lost treasure of Pecos Canyon

Webb County (Aguilares): Buried treasure of Eagles' Nest

Young County: Bandit treasure of old Fort Belknap, Spanish mission treasure

Zavala County (Crystal City): Lost treasure of Espantosa Lake

UTAH

Box Elder County (western): Lost Bidwell treasure

Grand County (Grand Valley): Train robber's treasure

  (Sagers): Lost treasure of the Japanese Cook

Kane County (Kanab): Montezuma's treasure of White Mountain

Tooele County (Silver Island): Lost Donner Party treasure

VERMONT

Addison County (Bristol): Buried treasure of Hell's Half Acre

Bennington County (Bennington): Lost British treasure

Essex County (Essex): Spanish treasure of Winooski Valley

Franklin County (St. Albans): St. Albans raid treasure

Orleans County (Lake Memphremagog): Lost treasure of Providence Island

Washington County (Waterbury): Lost treasure of Camel's Hump

Windham County (Bellows Falls): Captain Kidd's buried treasure

(White Hills): Pagan treasure of St. Francis

(Whitingham): Buried pirate treasure

VIRGINIA

Henrico County (Richmond): Buried Confederate treasure

Rockingham County (McGaheysville): Peaked Mountain buried treasure

WASHINGTON

Asotin County (Rogersburg): Prospector's buried treasure

Discovery Bay area: British paymaster's buried treasure

Stevens County (Fruitland): Robber's Roost treasure

Vashon Island: Lars Hanson lost treasure

WEST VIRGINIA

Berkeley County (Potomac River vicinity): Grover Bergdoll treasure

WISCONSIN

Apostle Islands: Hermit treasure of Wilson Island (Sand Island): British soldier's treasure

Iowa County (Arena): Indian treasure cave

Oneida County (Rhinelander): John Dillinger's buried treasure

Richland County (Orion): Buried treasure of Bogus Bluff

Winnebago County: Buried Swamp treasure

WYOMING

Crook County (Black Hills): Canyon Springs Stage robbery treasure

Jackson Hole country: Bandit treasure

Platte County (Guernsey): Buried treasure of Sawmill Canyon

Sublette County (Big Piney): Paymaster's lost treasure

Teton County (Jackson): Stage robbery treasure

Wind River Mountains: Butch Cassidy's buried bandit loot